Deformed, Disfigured, And Despised

First Lesson Sermons
For Lent/Easter
Cycle C

Carlyle Fielding Stewart III

CSS Publishing Company, Inc., Lima, Ohio

Library of Congress Cataloging-in-Publication Data

Stewart, Carlyle Fielding, 1951-
  Deformed, disfigured and despised-a marred but magnificent Messiah : first lesson
sermons for Lent/Easter, cycle C / Carlyle Fielding Stewart.
      p. cm.
  ISBN 0-7880-1716-0 (alk. paper)
    1. Lenten sermons. 2. Easter—Sermons. 3. Bible. O.T.—Sermons. 4. Bible. N.T. Acts—
Sermons. 5. Sermons, American. 6. Lectionary preaching. I. Title.
BV4277 .S785 2000
252'.62—dc21   00-035791
                                                                                             CIP

This book is available in the following formats, listed by ISBN:
    0-7880-1716-0   Book
    0-7880-1717-9   Disk
    0-7880-1718-7   Sermon Prep

For more information about CSS Publishing Company resources, visit our website at
www.csspub.com.

*"At that time also there appeared
a certain man of magic power —
if it is meet to call him a man — whom
certain Greeks call a son of a God,
but his disciples, the true prophet
who is supposed to have raised dead persons
and to have cured all diseases.*

*Both his nature and form were human,
for he was a man of simple appearance,
mature age, dark skin,
short growth, three cubits tall,
hunchbacked with a long face,
a long nose,
eyebrows meeting above the nose
so that spectators could take fright,
with scanty hair but having a line in the middle of the head
after the fashion of the Nazareans
and with an undeveloped beard."*

*Flavius Josephus
Halosis*

*"But I am a worm, and not a man,
scorned by men and despised by the people."*

Psalm 22:6

*"He had no beauty or majesty to attract us to him,
nothing in his appearance that we should desire him.
He was despised and rejected by men,
a man of sorrows, and familiar with suffering.
Like one from whom men hide their faces
he was despised, and we esteemed him not."*

Isaiah 53:2b-3

Table Of Contents

Introduction

These Lenten sermons are a tribute to Jesus Christ, our Lord, Savior, and liberator; our marred but magnificent Messiah. This image of an ugly and scorned Messiah may contradict artistic portraits and renderings depicting our Lord as venerable, handsome, and attractive. First-century Christian communities knew Jesus to be uncomely, a man who drew unto himself the despised, afflicted, and rejected not only because he could heal their maladies, but also because there was something about his visage and form that compelled these people to identify with him. So marred and unbeautiful was he that those who were like him were drawn to him, and he changed their lives forever. To come into his presence and even touch the hem of his garment would give them hope, power, physical healing, and spiritual renewal. They too could transcend the problems and plight of their own condition and live as free and accepted persons in Christ.

Since the first century, historical descriptions of Jesus have changed quite drastically. Many generations, cultures, and peoples have portrayed Christ according to their own icons, conceptions, and perceptions. In contemplating this man of sorrows, who had his own physical afflictions, the most cumbersome of which may have been spinal kyphosis, and who took upon himself our sorrows and sins to save and redeem us, we too reel in astonishment. That he would have his own afflictions, and not cure himself, and then give his own life to save us is both incredible and miraculous.

Given his own possible spinal curvature, which was a common malady of carpenters and artisans who worked long hours in stooped positions and prompted enormous pain, it is even more remarkable that he would walk long distances in his ministry, that

7

he would bear his own cross, hang on the cross for hours, and endure at the hands of his enemies inordinate, interminable, and insufferable humiliation and abuse.

Jesus' capacity to overcome life's physical challenges and complexities to do the work of his Father is a tribute both to his commitment to save us and his towering strength as the anointed Son of God. Not only did he have no form of comeliness that we should behold him but he may have had his own share of physical challenges that made his life physically vexing and torturous.

Lent is thus a time of remembering the sacrifices, suffering, and triumph of our Lord. We as followers of Jesus the Christ and heirs of his legacy have been granted the same spirit of victory. We cannot then, as followers of Christ, have great expectations of Christ and low expectations of ourselves. Even in our foibles, infirmities, and ugliness, Christ empowers us to overcome and press on toward the prize of his high calling through an undaunted and unvanquishable faith.

Christ paid the price for us with his life. Recall too that he was marred, unwanted, unattractive, but magnificent in the way that he surmounted the forces of evil and cemented the forces of light to give us new life. That same Christ lives today, saves today, and is alive and well today.

Let us then pay tribute to him. Let us give honor and glory to him in all things so that the Father will be magnified, the Son will be glorified, the Holy Ghost will be verified, believers will be edified, and Satan will be horrified.

He is marred but magnificent! He was uncomely but overcame our infirmities and shortcomings through his sacrifice. He was despised but gave us entry into the elect of God. All praises due to a marred but magnificent messiah.

I pray that these sermons will be a source of power, hope, and inspiration for those who read them. They are tributes to our Lord. All praises due our Lord and Savior, Christ our King, who gave his life that we might have eternal life.

With All
Your Heart

Joel 2:1-2, 12-17

The poignant words of the prophet Joel should have deep relevance and meaning for this Ash Wednesday, for it is a clarion call to remembrance and reflection. The prophet calls the people to repentance and urges a sincere return to God. The various passages of the prophet's entire oracle to Judah, whose language is reminiscent of Isaiah, Obadiah, Zephaniah, Malachi, and Jeremiah in their reference to the "Day of the Lord," "the enemy from the North," and "judgment on foreign nations," contains a heightened sense of urgency for the people of God. Joel's lament is that the day of the Lord is coming. Such events in ancient times had portended "seismic disturbances" of disastrous proportions. The prophet's warning contains elements of pessimism and hope, despair and joy. The people have been fairly warned, but will they return to God with all their hearts?

The opening passages of chapter two bewail the "day of darkness and gloom and the day of clouds and blackness that are approaching." The symbolism is both literal and figurative. Dark clouds hover on the landscape of Judah, for the land itself has experienced a kind of degradation and desolation, and the people's hearts are black with the darkness of their apostasy, iniquity, and spiritual defection. The land itself is permeated with clouds of gloom and the soulscape of their hearts is besmirched by sin. "Blow the Trumpet in Zion, and sound the alarm ... return to me with all your heart."

The prophet exhorts a return to God "with all your heart." The heart was believed to possess the same power and influence over

9

the souls and wills of people as the brain is believed today. The heart was the seat of sentiment and intellect, will and determination. If the people return to God with all their hearts, then their return will at once be final and complete. They had simulated return in previous generations according to the Covenants but not with all their hearts.

God wants the return of his people in mind, body, soul, and spirit. Lent is a season for return, a time for remembering and reflecting, a time for positive transformation and renewal. Ash Wednesday is the beginning of the Lenten season and God wants us to do more than rent our garments and give up other habits and addictions. More importantly, God wants us to return to him with all our hearts.

For transformation to become full and deep, we must first return to God with a heart of acknowledgement and remembrance. How often we forget what God has done and what God has promised to those who love him? Our memories are short. Our patience is thin. We immerse ourselves in the daily round of life, preoccupy ourselves with living and dying, amuse ourselves with the gadgets and trinkets of our modern culture, bemuse our things with the irrelevancies and trivialities of life, and leave God out, except in emergencies.

The great tragedy of our times is living as though God did not exist, as though God were not responsible for our largesse and success. The tragedy of our times is the way in which we crowd God out of our daily affairs, the way that we leave God out in our remembrance, and the way that life and living intercept us from God. Who will return with a heart of acknowledgment, remembrance, and gratitude?

Even more tragic is how the terrors of life take us away from an acknowledgement of the one who gives us life and eternal life. Sorrow and tribulation, trial and difficulty often cast their spells over us, mesmerize and possess, stifle and anesthetize us to the things that God has done for us. Our memories can be easily filled with the things that God has not done, and our hearts become cynical and resentful, and we turn away from God. Is it not God who gives us life? Is it not God who has given us his Son so that we might have life and have it abundantly? Why then must we turn from the hand that keeps us, saves us, comforts and renews us? A return to God with all our hearts means returning to God with a heart of acknowledgment and remembrance of God's many blessings and the ways he has brought and kept us along this way. If the people of God can remember what God has done in the past, they can anticipate what God will do in the future.

Second, we must return to God with a heart of confession. Sin hardens our hearts and seduces us into a routinization which alienates us from God. Sin has its own initiation rites, its own mantra, its own methods of physical seduction and spiritual reduction which prevent us from having a heart that is willing to confess.

Confessing our sin unloads the burden of sin, unyokes the reigns of sin, unleashes the energy of sin, uncages the guilt of sin, unbinds the sorrow of sin, unearths the causes of sin, and unnerves the power of sin. Sin creates its own patterns of domestication and subordination that solidifies its dominion and reinforces its hegemony in our lives. Confessing our sin is subverting sin's power and authority, sin's legal right to take up residency in our hearts and souls, the rulership and governance of sin in our lives. Confessing our sin is a declaration of war against sin's providence and devastations. Confessing our sin seeks the eviction of sin from permanent habitation in our hearts, minds, and souls.

1 John 1:8-9, reminds us, "If we claim to be without sin, we deceive ourselves and the truth is not in us. If we confess our sins, he is faithful and just and will forgive our sins and purify us from all unrighteousness." God wants a heart that confesses sin because God likes an honest heart, a contrite heart, a heart that is willing to reveal its imperfections and afflictions.

Third, we must return to God with a heart of repentance. Repenting means acknowledging, confessing, and turning away from sin. Repentance is the act of contrition carried out to cancel sin's transgression. To say we have sinned is one thing. To turn away from sinful ways is quite another thing. God wants a repenting heart. A heart that is open to being used by God to set new directions for the future. The conviction of sin causes an action that renounces and turns away from sin. Repenting of sin is turning toward God for resolution and deliverance from the conditions of sin.

The heart that acknowledges God, confesses its sin, and returns to God in word and action is truly a heart that God is seeking. Actually to turn away in thought and deed is to return to God for life, power, and strength. But it is difficult to repent without faith, without a desire to love and please God. It is difficult to repent if the conscience has not been convicted of wrongdoing. It is difficult to repent when sin habituates the mind and eviscerates the heart's desire to get right with God. God wants a heart of repentance that leads to redemption.

God wants to turn us around from the ways of sin. God wants to turn us around from evil, hatred, malice, and malevolence. God wants us to turn to him in body, mind, spirit, and soul. Repentance is an expression of the soul's and heart's desire to turn things around for God, through God, and by God.

Fourth, God wants a heart of redemption; a heart of love and forgiveness, compassion and understanding; a heart that is willing to redeem others and be redeemed.

A heart of love and compassion is what it is all about. Sin and a lack of love harden the heart. God loves us and we are a called to love others. God so loved the world that he sent his son to us out of love, and we as followers of Christ should spread the Good News of love in a world filled with resentment and hatred.

God wants to redeem his people. God wants his people to have a heart and spirit of redemption for others. The people of Joel's time were hurting from their past. Some of them had lost all hope of ever achieving the spiritual greatness of their forbears. But God always sees new possibilities amid the disabilities of our human condition. God is always making a way out of no way, seeking ways of restoring his people to spiritual wholeness, health, and vitality. No situation is so hopeless that God cannot redemptively work his will toward renewal and restoration.

That is why he sent us his son, who died for us and to redeem us. All at times appears to be hopeless, but God is still holding for that day of truth when the people of God will return to him with all their hearts. This is the season of return, restoration, and renewal. A season of hope and joy, comfort and celebration, for a comforter has come to lay down his life for those who are seeking life. It is not enough to rent our clothes, to give up old habits and bad ways; we must return to him with all our hearts so that we his people may renew our souls. Return to me, oh people, with all your heart! Return to me!

Not Your Leftovers But Your First Fruits

Deuteronomy 26:1-11

In the text, Moses exhorts the people to offer unto God their first fruits in remembrance and thanksgiving for their inheritance of the new land. They have toiled and struggled in the wilderness for many years and have come at long last to the place of divine promise. God has been good to them. God has kept his promises and has brought them to a place of great wealth and prosperity. The soil is ripe for planting and harvesting. The hills and valleys are rich with minerals. The water flows like milk and foliage tastes of honey. The sky is blue, the grass is green, and the earth is good. Unlike the wilderness whose harsh terrain, lurking dangers, and arid places punish, maim, and discourage God's people, the new land is warm and embracing and full of promise of new life.

Moses asks the people to remember the blessings of their God and to honor God with the first fruits of their labors. This is a fitting tribute to a God who has stood by them, kept them largely from harm's way, and preserved a remnant who could carry forth the dreams and aspirations of their mothers and fathers who perished en route to the new land. A proper honor is to offer God their first fruits and not their leftovers.

Moses here is setting the spiritual priorities of the new people in the new land. God must be honored first, for it is God, very God, who has saved them and kept them, promised and renewed them in their painstaking quest for the new frontier. God gave them the soil, the seed, the will, and the desire to plant and grow. God gave them the sun and the rain, the wind and the stars to nurture and keep watch over them. God, then, must be honored with their first

15

fruits and not their leftovers. God must be placed first in all things because it is the mercy, grace, providence, and power of God that makes their survival possible and their dreams achievable.

How often today do we give God our leftovers and not our first fruits? God wants our first fruits.

First, we must give God more than our leftover thoughts and thinking. After many years of thinking or after occasional crises or in 911 situations, we think of God only in terms of what he can do for us now and seldom of what we can do for God now and forever. "God," for some, in the words of Harry Emerson Fosdick, is nothing more than "a cosmic bellhop." We push the button and call his name out only when we need him, but seldom make reference to him, respect or praise him, or give him our first thoughts of each waking day.

We have not prioritized God in our thinking. We have not made God the ultimate index and reference point for all that we have and all that we do. Our thoughts of God are leftover from our other more important thoughts. These divine thoughts emerge "after everything else." They are thoughts of getting and spending, buying and having, needing and wanting. We have not prioritized God in our thinking and doing, so as to give God praise and thanks for the things he has done and does each day.

We fail to remember to thank God for such things as peaceful rest, the fresh air we breathe, the life we have, the food we eat, the health we enjoy, the smell of fresh flowers, the smiles of children, and the laughter of other people. Our thinking is too horizontal. We need to orient ourselves vertically in the things of God. If we prioritize God in our thinking, God will be more than a leftover thought, and we would give God the first fruits of our minds and our thinking. We would reference God, praise God, and thank God for his many blessings. A great tragedy in our time, said one writer, is not to ignore, deny or negate God, but to live as though God never existed.

In the days of Moses, the people understood the bounty, mercy, and grace of God. In largely agrarian and nomadic communities, dependence on God and acknowledgement of God was direct, for it was God who gave rain and sun. It was God who gave strength to till the soil, and God who steadied weary steps that walked great distances. It was God who provided the very sustenance that germinated the crops to grow and gave human energy and strength for the harvest.

Moses underscores the importance of the people placing God first in their thinking, for prioritized thinking of God will lead to prioritized action on behalf of God.

Second, we must give God more than our leftover time. God gives us 168 hours per week. How much of that week do we spend in Bible study, devotion, prayer, service to others in the church, fasting, and other spiritual disciplines? We give God time we have left over after everything else has been done. God gives us our most precious resource, which is time, yet we can find little time for God. "Everything intercepts us from ourselves," says Ralph Waldo Emerson. We spend our lives in the daily round of getting, doing, and going so that we can scarcely find time for God, to sit in silent meditation and to pray fervent, joyous, or simple prayers. The fury of the present age crowds God out of our daily routine so we have little or no time for God. Yet when we need God we expect him to be Johnny-on-the-spot. We make no time for him, yet expect him to give us our undivided attention when we need it!

We spend a lifetime serving the gods and idols of the larger culture. We worship our material possessions, bow down to the emperors in new clothes, believe that money is God, and give only condescending reference to the possibilities of God. We do not give God the first fruits of our time. We spend our time in concert halls, malls, and dance halls, ballparks, theme parks, and water parks, bars, movie theaters, and golf courses, pursuing amusements and bemusements. Not that we should not have a good time; not that we should not enjoy ourselves. But what about God? What about the God who gives us life and eternal life, the God who makes this life of enjoyment possible? Some of us spend more time in front of the television, flicking the remote control, than we do seeking his word and his kingdom. Where are our priorities? Because God is an afterthought, we might give God our left over time after everything else in our lives.

Out of 168 hours a week, how much time do we spend in devotion, Bible study, prayer, fellowshiping with the saints, and serving others in the church? How much time do we spend worshiping, singing, praising, and listening to God? One writer said we spend as much time with God as the national anthem before a sports event and our reference to God is like the national anthem. It gets things started but is never referred to again throughout the event. We acknowledge God in starting our day but never make reference to him throughout our day.

Giving God the first fruits of our time means giving God praise in the morning and praise at night. It means setting aside our precious time in service to someone else in the name of God. It means disciplining ourselves to seek God in all things and to devote ourselves to studying his word and strengthening the body of Christ in ways that will empower others and give God glory. We must give God more than the leftovers of our time. Can we not give God some of our temporal time, especially when he gives us eternal time through his Son?

Third, we must give God more than our leftover money and resources for kingdom building. Some people treat God like the paperboy. The paperboy is one of the only persons to give us service on a daily basis but is often the last one paid. Everyone else gets paid first, but the paperboy who is up bright and early every morning, faithfully bringing the newspaper to read over breakfast and coffee, is often the last one paid.

Some people treat God the same way. They pay everyone else first. They give their money to the mortgage company, automobile and clothing manufacturers, retail outlets, and superstores. They pay 25 percent interest on credit cards to banks and fifteen percent tips for lousy service and horrible-tasting food at restaurants. They give enormous sums of money to state lotteries, casinos, liquor and tobacco companies, and hair dressers. They spend a fortune on false fingernails, wigs, pedicures, manicures, bowl tickets, and other things, and complain when they are asked to tithe to God's church. They enjoy their lives and pay everyone else and just give God and his church credit for all the good things God has done for them.

God wants more than our credit. God wants our first fruits. God wants the first fruit of our tithes.

Why in the midst of unsurpassed prosperity and a booming economy should God's church go wanting and begging just to subsist and survive? Because the people have not offered God the first fruits of their earnings but their leftovers after everyone else has been paid.

During our first capital stewardship campaign, one man complained that the church was always asking for money. I begged to differ from his assessment. I replied, "Everyone else wants money. The world is always begging for money. The world charges you for everything and the church seldom does. For example, you go to the grocery store and buy your food. You come to the church and eat free. You go the psychiatrist for counseling and pay 100 dollars an hour for therapy. But you come to the church and receive pastoral counseling for nothing. You pay for direct television and cable to access the televangelists and come to the church and get a free sermon. You send all your money to the televangelists and give nothing to your local church. Yet if you want counseling or want to bury a family member, you go to the local church. You send all your money to the televangelists while your local church goes wanting and begging. The church is not always asking for money. The world always has its hand out wanting you to pay for what you get. The church seldom asks you to pay for anything you get. But when the church asks for money you exclaim that the church is always begging!"

But why should God's church go wanting and begging? Why should preachers and leaders even have to ask members to give to the church? If every member tithed by giving his first fruits the church would never have to beg members to give to the cause of Christ. If God is truly first in our lives, why are so many ministries suffering from lack of finances? "Will a man rob God? You rob me in tithes and offerings," says God!

Moses understood the value of challenging the people to remember whence cometh their bread and butter. He was forthright and direct in urging the people to bring their first fruits and not their leftovers for God.

God gives us the best of everything he has to offer. He gave us his son. He gives us life and health and vitality. He gives us the earth, the sky, and the trees. He gives us tools with which to till the soil and bring forth produce to feed our families. Were it not for the mercy, grace, love, and sustenance of God we would have nothing. Therefore it is a fitting tribute to our God, to his church, and to his ministry to bring the first fruits of the harvest — the first fruits of our income, the first fruits of our time, and the first fruits of our thoughts. For if we prioritize God in these three things we can continue the prosperity that God has called us into. We should give God our first fruits and not our leftovers, for the Lord should be first in all that we give and do for kingdom building in his name. God says, "Don't give me your leftovers. Give me your first fruits!"

The Promise Of A Son

Genesis 15:1-12, 17-18

A son was a symbol of the strength of the inheritance. A son would carry on the family name and continue the family line. A son represented the promises of a realizable future amid clear and present dangers. A son would be the embodiment of hope and opportunity for future generations. A son would understand the meaning of sacrifice, fortitude, vision, and courage. Abram wanted a son so he could place his mantle upon him.

Here was a man whose faith had been tested. He set out as a man of 75 years to leave his country and his people to herald a new land and to become the father of a new people. He traveled into Canaan and received the promise of God that this land would one day be his land, and Abram, stepping out on faith, trusted and believed in God.

Because of famine, he went into Egypt. Because of the fear of his own death, he lied about Sarai being his sister instead of his wife. He saw Pharaoh afflicted and was set free, thereby escaping from Egypt with his wife and his life. He later rescued Lot from four kings who had captured him, made promises to God to keep his word, and gave to God a tenth of everything he had. Getting too old for all this adventure, and tired of being a high-plains drifter, he settled down for a time on the plains of Shaveh, still keeping watch and holding on to the promises of God.

Finally, God came to Abram in a vision with a promise that he would have a son who would be his heir who would come from his own body, more than the promise of the covenant, more than the promise of the new land, more than the promise of prosperity and protection, the promise of a son bolstered his hopes and renewed his energy and strength. The promise of all promises would be a son that would be born from the body of a man and woman who were past the age of childbirth. It was the promise of a son that cheered Abram and quickened his resolve to press on into the future. If God could lead him into a land he could not imagine, and give him a people to lead who were not yet in existence, God could give him a son he did not have. God, then, would do the impossible and make that impossibility a reality through the gift of his promises.

God does not break his promises. God makes good on his promises. If God promises something, we can trust that God will bring it to fruition.

The promise of a son would then secure Abram's legacy of faith. Birthrights included inheritances that made provisions for the firstborn sons and other sons. Inheritances of physical possessions were very important, particularly in nomadic communities where lurking dangers threatened long-term hopes and the future. An endowment could be fleeced away in the twinkling of an eye by roving and marauding bandits. More important was the inheritance of a spiritual legacy, a legacy of absolute trust and faith in God. More important for Abram was a legacy of faith that he could bequeath to his son, because faith is more precious than gold. Abram understood that faith in God is the quintessential gift of our power, our value, and our resourcefulness. A son would carry forth this legacy and share it with his people. This faith would be the cornerstone of a new nation and a new people.

The promise of a son would symbolize hope for the future. In Abram's time a fundamental question was asked: "Will I have a son to carry on my legacy and secure hope for future generations?" What good is that land without a son? What good is an inheritance without a son? What good is the present without hope for tomorrow?

A son would secure the future because he carries and transmits the seed of future generations. A son would realize the hopes, dreams, and visions of both predecessors and posterity. A son would embody and articulate the covenant promises of God's people. A son would make the necessary sacrifices for family and people and nation to move them forward. A son could instill within future generations the strong values of the past.

God sent us his son, Jesus, so that we might have a future hope that cannot be vanquished by the sorrows and trials of our lives. Our hope is in Christ, the son who gives to us the power to look upward and outward for a better day.

Do you have a legacy of hope for future generations and those who will come behind you? Do you have a seed that will bear the imprint of hope for future generations? A son promised hope for the future!

The promise of a son would mean God's continuing favor. The intent here is not to sound sexist, but the ancients believed that sons were directly a sign of God's favor for health, wealth, and prosperity of their families. So long as Abram was without a son, he could question God's approval of his faith and obedience to God. Doubts about God's affirmation could still linger, but God knew that Abram desired a son and granted him the desire of his heart. What Abram needed was confirmation that God was pleased with his faithfulness. The birth of his own son would thus be a sign of God's continuing favor of Abram's obedience, commitment, and faithfulness to God's vision and promises for his life and his people.

We look for signs of approval. We look for corroborating evidence and proofs that we are doing what pleases God. We seek some external confirmation that God is in favor of all that we do for him.

As Christians, we believe that God has sent us his son not only as a sign of God's continuing favor to his people, but also to secure our future and to preserve and strengthen our legacy of faith through him. Jesus, the son, was sent by the father as a sign of God's continuing favor to us. But unlike Abram who was wholly deserving of his son because of his faithfulness and obedience to God, we have not always been deserving, but it is out of God's love and concern for us that he sent us his son to give us eternal life.

For Abram, the son and his seed would continue for eternity. For Christians, the son Jesus and his seed give us eternal life. It is the promise that God makes to give that son that secures our hope, solidifies our faith, and tells us of God's continuing favor.

We sinners are imperfect and flawed, like Abram, but the promise of the son and the gift of God's son is a sign of redemption and hope. That God would love us so much that he would give his only son is continuation of that covenant promise he made to his people many generations ago.

The gift of Abram is God's promise of a son and the establishment of a covenant whose promises God would keep. The gift of Christians is what his son Jesus promises through the establishment of a new covenant. God promises to give Abram a son as a sign of God's continuing favor and prosperity. God gives us a son who promises to fulfill all that God has promised through his spiritual lineage.

The promise of a son cheered Abram, renewed his strength, and bolstered his confidence in the future. The son Jesus Christ promises Christians a strength and power that will help them face the future. It is therefore not only the promise of a son but what the son promises that gives us confidence and faith for the future as Christians and as spiritual heirs of the legacy of Abram.

While He May Be Found

Isaiah 55:1-9

Isaiah issues a four-part injunction to the people of Judah to return to God, to renounce their iniquities, and to reaffirm the promises of the Davidic Covenant: come (55:1), listen (55:2), seek, and call on God while he is near and can be found (55:6). This plea is pertinent to Christians during this season of Lent, a season of exile and return, renewal and restoration, affliction and comfort, and death and resurrection.

The prophet exhorts us to *come* unto the Lord. The prophet urges them to "come" and turn from their crooked and wicked ways. "Come all who are thirsty ... and you who have no money, come, buy and eat! Come, buy wine and milk without money and without cost" (55:1).

It does not cost the sinner to come to God, for he can receive the gift of salvation without cost. He can purchase what he does not have and eat what he cannot afford. Come, poor sinner! Come now while the opportunity is near! Come now while the Lord may be found! Time is running out. The opportunities to come may not always be here. Drop everything and come to the Lord. Do not wait and do not hesitate, for tomorrow is not promised!

See the ill-clad prophet in the town square at Jerusalem, standing on a rickety platform, sweating, exhorting, preaching, and pleading with the people to come unto the Lord. Some pause to hear him. Others are busy with their business. Still others completely dismiss him. He issues an open invitation, a warning, to come unto God and receive the gifts that God has to offer.

Money is not a qualification to come to the Lord. If you are thirsty, you can come. If you are hungry, you can come. If you are lonely, you can come. If you are sorrowful, you can come. If you are heartbroken, you can come. If you are poor and oppressed, rich and prosperous, you can come. Your social status or station should not prevent you from coming to the Lord, for God will put food on your table, will give you milk to drink, and will satisfy your soul. But how will you know if you do not come? How will you taste and see if you never come unto the Most High who calls you unto him? How will you know if you do not heed the invitation to come unto him? Your soul will delight in riches. Your soul will live if you come, my people!

Come, poor sinner. Come to church. Come into the body of Christ and the koinonia of the ecclesia. Come, all ye who labor and are heavy laden and I will give you rest. Come, poor sinner, to the cross of Christ. Come to the grave of Christ. Come to the tomb of Christ. Come to Gethesemane and Golgotha. Come to the living waters. Come to the desert valleys. Come to the table of life. Come to the Lord of life and see what he will do with your life!

But are we too busy to come? Too preoccupied with our lifestyles, responsibilities, and other concerns to come? But it is precisely we who need to come and return unto God for salvation.

The prophet urges us to come and listen to God's word. Hear the word, oh sinner. Could it be that we are tired of hearing? The words of the prophet burn our ears and wrench our hearts. But if we come and listen, we can be changed. If we come and listen, we can be saved. If we come and hear the word of God, it can penetrate our minds and hearts, our bodies and souls, and we can receive the gift of salvation. "How shall they hear without someone preaching to them?" (Romans 10:14c). Listen and hear, oh people of God, for your soul will delight in the richest of fare and your soul may live.

We have grown tired of hearing. Our souls are saturated with the noise of the world, the cacophony of daily living. We hear the music. The constant sounds from our television and radios drown out the serenity of the soul. We hear the news which is mostly bad. Our days are filled with the clamor of the world around us. We hear the clanging of the world constantly blasting in our ears, and we become tired and sick of listening and hearing.

One friend, in an effort to escape the noise of the world, loves to go parasailing. It's the only place in the world where you can go where there is absolute silence. Suspended in midair over the ocean, there are no sounds, just silence.

The word of God brings silence, tranquility, and renewal. It also brings anxiety, affliction, and discomfort. It is fresh and cleansing, like music to the soul. Hear the word of God, and it will give comfort to the afflicted and it will afflict the comfortable. It will give sight to the blind, hope to the hopeless, and joy to the joyless. If you are down, it will pick you up. If you are lost, you will be found. If you need affirmation and restoration, it will restore your soul.

Listen and hear the word of God. Listening is something we don't do well in this culture. We hear what we want to hear. We see what we want to see. We hear others not as they are but as we are. People talk at each other. The drama and trauma of daily living anesthetizes our senses so that we cannot hear. We cannot hear because we are tired of hearing. We cannot hear because we have heard it all before. We cannot hear because we are on sensory overload. We cannot hear because it cuts us to the core, offends us, and turns us off. We cannot hear because our souls are lost in the babble and pandemonium of life. We drone and drown each other out. We tune each other out, and we no longer possess the desire to hear what the other has to say. But hearing and listening are still the two most important acts of communication. To listen and hear another is saying to them that they are important.

God speaks to his people because they are important. The people hear what God has to say because God is important. What can be more important than listening to what the prophet must say on behalf of the Lord? What can be more important than hearing the word of God which runs like fresh waters through our souls? The people have shut God out and God is not pleased with the ways they have chosen to ignore and dismiss him.

The prophet urges the people to *seek* the Lord while he may be found and *call* upon him while he is near.

The great Karl Barth tells us that man does not find God, but God finds man. But there must be a mutual seeking. Whatever you are looking for is looking for you. We must seek God, pursue God's presence, invoke God's spirit, and celebrate God's joy and power.

What happens to a people who no longer seek God or a people who believe God is no longer worth seeking? The people are no longer hungry, no longer poor, no longer broken. Not having something can prompt a man to seek for something with all his heart and soul. Have we in our modern culture lost our hunger and desire for seeking God? We seek pleasure. We seek enjoyment and entertainment. We seek rest and relaxation. We seek money and power. We seek sex and satisfaction. We seek recognition and fame, but do we seek God? Do we take God for granted? Have we lost touch with the real needs that compel us on bended knees into God's presence?

The prophet is aware of the arrogance and disdain that the people have for God. They have basked in their fortunes and have lived the good life and have not sought God. They have experienced poverty of the body and spirit and have not sought God. While they enjoy the amenities of the good life, their souls teeter on the brink of disaster and desolation. They prosper materially and squander spiritually. They reach the pinnacle of social success but cower in the dungeons of spiritual despair.

The answer is to seek God while he may be found and call on him while he is near. We must not take for granted God's availability and omnipresence. Time is running out. Our sin and iniquity paralyze us from truly seeking God in all things. We have become weary and complacent. We have given up our seeking. But it is precisely because of our pursuit of God and God's presence that we can be restored, renewed, and saved from the pestilence that cripples our seeking.

If we truly seek him, he can be found. If we do not seek him, we may lose our way. If we seek him, we can find joy, happiness, peace, prosperity, and a renewal of life. If we seek him and call upon him, he can answer our prayers, quicken our resolve, bolster our faith, renew our trust in him, stymie our afflictions, stifle our opposition, steady our steps, refurbish our strength, and restore our desire to be with him, dwell in him, and seek him in all things.

Seeking him means confessing our sin, admitting our faults, and finding the path that leads into God's presence. It means a staying on the path when life and circumstances try to throw us off that path. It means getting up after being knocked down to the ground, and giving him praise and glory for the trials we've overcome and the victories we have won.

The prophet has a perfect formula for spiritual renewal and restoration. If we come, listen, seek, and call on him, he will answer our prayers and grant us the desires of our hearts and restore our faith and confidence as his people. We can defeat the spiritual famine which threatens the destruction of our very souls. He will quench our thirst and remove our hunger if we seek and call on him. All this can be offered without cost.

Come, listen, seek, and call on the Lord while he may be found! Come to him, O sinner. Come to him, you who are weary. Come to him, you who are lost. Come to the Lord that he may renew your strength and give you joy for the living of these days!

Reproach
Rolled Away

Joshua 5:9-12

After wandering in the wilderness 39 years, braving many dangers, toils, and snares, and after watching a generation of their mothers and fathers perish in the wilderness, the Hebrews celebrate the first Passover in the Promised Land. This is the third Passover since their last at the foot of Mount Sinai. The first Passover they hovered in fear as they ate their unleavened bread, roasted lamb, and bitter herbs and prayed to God in hope that the blood of sacrifice which marked the door frames of their homes would allow God to pass them over and spare their firstborn sons from the plague of death. Now they were preparing for a Passover where they would eat more than the hurried meal and which would not be eclipsed by the lengthening shadows of fear and terror that marked their earlier celebrations.

Now they could eat in peace. Now they could anticipate movement into the new land because the reproach of Egypt was rolled away. The rebuke, scorn, and denigration of their former captors would melt away with the morning sun. Reproach was finally rolled away. All the previous years of hardship, toil, and struggle through faithfulness would now evaporate like the morning dew. What a beautiful moment it is when reproach is finally rolled away, when victory finally comes, when the joy of conquest of the new land finally occurs! The people could now stand tall with their backs straight and heads high, knowing in their hearts and souls that God gave them the victory through and through. This is the moment of truth. This is the moment of a true declaration of spiritual independence.

31

Reproach is therefore rolled away when God gives the victims victory over their victimizers.

In Egypt the Hebrews were victims of Pharaoh's wrath and oppression. They were forced to make bricks without straw, were treated cruelly, and suffered to work long hours with very little sleep and very little food. They were oppressed physically, mentally, and spiritually. Many of them perished from overwork and undernourishment. Scorned, despised, and rejected, they were the wretched of the earth and many of them had lost all hope of ever being liberated from Pharaoh's hand.

But while many of them were oppressed and victimized by the terror and tyranny of Pharaoh, they still kept hope and faith that they would one day be delivered from their plight. While they were victimized by their victimizers, they did not develop a victim's mindset and outlook, a victim's condition and lament.

Some people who are victims continually live out their days without hope of ever being liberated and renewed from the ravages of their personal devastation. But you can be enslaved and yet avoid developing a slave's mentality. You can be victimized by life and calamities and cruelties but without developing a victim's outlook and state of mind that makes one forever the victimized.

Victims invariably view life in terms of what happened to them rather than what God can do in and for them. It is the pain and memory of being victimized unjustly by others that creates hatred, resentment, and even a desire to live without God. It is the experience of being victimized that can lead to a permanent condition of victimhood where the hope that redeems and heals is forever vanquished. Moving from victim to victor is knowing that the wounds of life can be healed, and that life, however fragile, can give wholeness. The great writer Elie Wiesel speaks well to the hope that compels the victims to claim victory over the victimizers. That hope is rooted in an irrepressible desire to maintain compassion and humanity in face of hatred and dehumanization and to maintain human dignity and integrity in the face of the forces of annihilation and despair.

Many of the Hebrews left Egypt with Moses because they no longer wanted to live as victims but wanted to claim sweet victory over their victimizers by denouncing oppression and permanently leaving Pharaoh's house. Some of the Hebrews carried the oppressors' image of them in their minds when some of them, after being sent to scout out the new land, exclaimed that it was impossible to conquer because they looked like grasshoppers in the eyes of their enemies. The mind and heart of the victim were further manifested in their desire to return to the ways and life of oppression in Egypt.

By stepping out in faith with Moses, they placed trust in God to deliver them from the havoc of personal oppression. Reproach was rolled away when they decided to live as victors and not victims.

Reproach is rolled away when wayward wanderers in the wilderness become serious sojourners and compliant conquerors of the Promised Land.

The Hebrews wandered in the wilderness longer than they needed to. They could have completed their journey in forty days but it took nearly forty years. Their disobedience, rebellion, and disdain for God and the leaders God appointed to liberate them caused them to be wayward wanderers in the wilderness. They complained, moaned, and instigated a rebellion against Moses. They wanted to return to the flesh pots of Egypt, turned to false idols, and were unruly, insolent, and at times intolerable. How quickly they forgot that it was God who delivered them from Pharaoh's hand. How quickly they sank into cantankerous contempt for all that God had done and promised to do. So they lost their spiritual focus and were unnerved by the hardships of wilderness life. God could have wiped them out entirely and canceled the trip because of their disobedience and rebellion. But God spared some of them while most of them perished because they wanted to remain wayward.

They provoked the anger and wrath of God on more than one occasion and were rebuked and blamed for their disorderly, impetuous, and rowdy unruliness. They once wandered waywardly and aimlessly in the wilderness. Now they would become serious sojourners with a purpose and a mission.

And now the Hebrews were poised to go into the Promised Land. After many years of suffering and wandering, moaning and

groaning, they were now ready to receive all that God had promised them. It was the obedience, faith, and experience of the younger
generation in the wilderness in watching their fathers and mothers
die, and the mercy and love of God that they were now ready to
receive God's promise of the new land faithfully. Now they would
become conquerors of the new land and no longer wayward wilderness wanderers. Now they would be compliant and do what
God had asked them to do forty years ago and take the new land
that God had promised.

Reproach is rolled away when they move from living by mo-
notonous manna to living by unleavened bread and the produce of
the new land.

They would no longer have to eat the unvaried diet of manna
alone, but God would give them produce from Canaan to fill their
bellies and satisfy their souls. This was the sign of God's favor.
They had circumcised their bodies and hearts, and they were now
ready to receive the abundance God had in store for them. God
rewards faithfulness with good fruit and produce that sustains the
body, mind, and soul. They would need new nourishment for the
conquest. They would need a full-course meal to strengthen them
for the fight. They had eaten their share of manna in the wilderness and now they could taste the goodness that God had in store
for them.

Now at Passover they could eat unleavened bread, grain, and
produce from the land. That they could eat it in a new land had as
much significance as the fact of their eating it. Unleavened bread
is much better than the dull sameness of the manna that was the
mainstay of the wilderness diet. It is bread without fermentation.
It is bread of the Passover symbolizing God's passing them over
and moving them through the Promised Land of their dreams.
That they could return to eating unleavened bread and celebrating
Passover signified a return to the the original promise of God to
continue their favor and spare their lives. Celebrating the Passover and discarding the bread of the wilderness meant the return
to the original promise of deliverance from Pharaoh. They were
grateful for having the opportunity to celebrate Passover once

again, but more happy with the savory taste of the new food that greeted their palates.

Reproach was rolled away for this people because of their dogged strength, faith, and determination coupled with God's grace and mercy. They would no longer dwell as slaves in Egypt and be blamed and castigated for their own oppression. They would no longer live as victims forever beholden to their victimizers but victors who would claim the promises of God. They would no longer wander waywardly in the wilderness but would become serious sojourners who could now have a home and food of their own that would nourish their bodies as they did God's work. God was pleased with their progress and decided to bless them as they prepared to settle in the new land.

When reproach is rolled away, we can live as victors. When reproach is rolled away, we no longer must live as wayward wanderers. When reproach is rolled away we eat new manna in a new land.

God rolls our reproach away as the stone was rolled away from the empty tomb. Today our reproach is rolled away by the love, grace, and mercy of Christ. The empty tomb is a symbol of our hope and promise for eternal life. The pain of our lament, the penalty of our sin, and the iniquity of our strife are rolled away by Christ Jesus. God rolls away the reproach of his people and calls them forth to claim the promise of a new day in glory!

When God Does
A New Thing

Isaiah 43:16-21

The woman whose heart is broken because her husband cheated on her cannot get past that experience and has vowed never to love again. Two brothers have not spoken to each other in years because a business they built together failed due to the skimming of profits by the older brother. The young man who has not visited or spoken to his mother and father in ten years because of an abusive childhood cannot bring himself to forget the past, forgive his parents, and move on with his life. These are just a few examples of people who cannot forget the former things and thus glimpse the new things God is doing in their lives.

The prophet Isaiah urges the people to forget the former things and behold the new ways that God is changing and renewing their lives for a greater good. But in order for them to see the new things that God is doing, they must open their eyes and see God. As human beings there are so many memories and experiences thwarting our movement into a fresh encounter with God. The windows of our hearts and souls are clouded with memories of the pain, hurt, and betrayal we have experienced over the years. But God wants to change all of that. God says, "Behold, I am doing a new thing. Will you not perceive it? Will you not know it? It springs up right before your very eyes. It is right before you. Can you not see it?" What new thing is God then doing in our lives?

God proclaims through the prophet, "I am making a way in the desert."

The desert is a lonely place where one can easily lose direction because of heat, fatigue, and disorientation. Even the most experienced desert guides have difficulty finding their way in the desert because of the terrain and the way desert conditions can easily discomfit and stymie the traveler. But God says, "I will make a way for you in the desert and you shall know the path I make for you and the path will lead you to fertile ground."

There also is the spiritual desert. A place of loneliness, misdirection, and confusion. Some people spend their lives wandering in the spiritual deserts of despair, disillusionment, and disappointment. Spiritual deserts can be encountered in our spiritual exile from God, where we feel estranged from the Lord and those who love us. We have lost our way. We are desert wanderers who have lost our focus and direction. We cannot find our way back to fertile ground.

Perhaps it is the desert of personal affliction and addiction. The alcoholic finds himself on the fallow ground of loneliness and denial where he cannot bring himself to admit that he is alcoholic. The same is true of the drug addict. He is lost in the vortex of drug abuse and finds his life spiraling out of control into the abyss of self destruction.

There are many people who have afflictions and addictions who have lost their way to God and cannot find their way back into God's presence.

The spiritual deserts are filled today with people who carry the baggage of their past and are wandering aimlessly on the hot sands of hopelessness and despair. The way out they have chosen for themselves is just a mirage. The only way out is by turning to God and away from those realities that keep them in the desert. The only way out is by taking God's hand and allowing God to lead them out. This involves admitting the problem, submitting to God, and committing to making positive personal transformation. God says, "I will make a way for you in the desert so you may find your way out of the desert."

God is also doing a new thing by making streams in the wasteland.

The wasteland is without fresh water. It is the place where dreams waste away. Hope and faith in God waste away. The great T. S. Eliot immortalized the wasteland with his poem:

Where is there an end of it ... the soundless wailing, the
silent withering of autumn flowers ... where is there an
end of the drifting wreckage ... the prayer of the bone
on the beach ... There is no end....

We live these days in spiritual wastelands where people have become so tainted and corrupt by the horrors and illusions of this age that they have lost all hope in God ever changing the present human condition. They resign themselves to eternal pessimism and have lost all belief in things ever getting better. They are permanent residents of spiritual wastelands. They are so steeped in the spiritual quagmires of the past that they cannot see God doing a new thing today. They live in wastelands where they waste away in body, mind, soul, and spirit. Their souls are arid. Their hearts have been dried out by the problems of society and living in general. Their minds have not been restored by the fresh waters of God's love, compassion, and mercy. They sit in their dry corners, parched offices, and barren boardrooms. They cower in their fallow and squalid places never understanding that God has made streams in the wasteland. If they would only look up and go to those fresh water places that God has created for their renewal, they would then see that God is doing a new thing in their midst.

This is also true of some churches which have become a kind of spiritual wasteland for our times. Some churches have lost much of their spiritual vitality and are suffering from spiritual dry rot. The church looks too much like the world and has sold its soul to the devil in an effort to imitate and accommodate the larger society. The same spiritual wasting away that we see in society and our Corinthian culture, we witness in the church where worship services are flat, dry, and vapid; where the singing and preaching are Geritol-tired, stale, perfunctory, and wooden, and the service is often devoid of the joy and enthusiasm that comes with genuine conversion to Christ. The church has also in many instances become a spiritual wasteland served by spiritual wastrels who have allowed the cynicism and problems of our post-modern secular culture to destroy and compromise their joy for Jesus. The sad irony is that certain sectors of the larger society have more faith in their institutions of power than the church has in Christ.

But God says, "I will make streams in the desert." The dry places shall become wet places. The old places shall become new places and the crooked places shall become straight places. That which has been eviscerated and evaporated of the streams of life shall be replenished and refurbished with the fresh, rushing waters of God's power and grace.

This is why God sent his son Jesus to this wasteland of ours — to give us hope, joy, and spiritual prosperity. God looked out over the world and saw what a waste we had made of things and decided to send his son who would clean things up and set things right. Where there is hopelessness, powerlessness, and joylessness, God will renew with hope, power, and joy. That which has been deemed impossible for humankind will be possible for God. We need not waste away on our porches of despair, rocking in confusion and disillusionment because God is doing a new thing even if we do not perceive it.

God says, "The wild animals honor me, even the jackals and the owls, because I provide water in the desert and streams in the wasteland." If the wild animals can perceive and acknowledge what God is doing, why can't humankind? If the animals who do not have the intelligence of humankind can see what God is doing, why can't humankind?

God is doing a new thing all around us. God is breaking down strongholds, transforming dark places into light places, and making hardened hearts into soft and compassionate hearts. God is giving wealth to the impoverished, bread to the hungry, water to the thirsty, hope to the hopeless, and faith to the faithless. God is doing a new thing everywhere. Tremendous advances in science and medicine have cured or halted many diseases that for years plagued and destroyed human communities. Walls that separate human communities are now being laid down and made into bridges. Those who were jailed unjustly are now heads of state. God is giving power to the powerless by setting the oppressed free. Everywhere we look we can see God doing a new thing, and if we look hard enough and discard the baggage and problems of the past that prevent us from seeing clearly, we can see clearly what God is doing.

Yes, problems still exist and man still faces his share of woe, but if the owls and jackals can see, why can't humankind see what God is doing? "Behold, I will do a new thing. Will you not perceive it? Behold I will do the impossible by making streams in the desert. I will give new life and new direction." The Father gives us something new in his son Jesus. Will we not perceive it and know what he can do in our lives? God is constantly doing new things through Christ who is the savior and liberator of the world. Deserts are made fertile. Crooked places are made straight and rough places are made plain. "Behold, I am doing a new thing!"

Sustaining The Weary With A Word

Isaiah 50:4-9a

Those who are beleagured can be strengthened by the prophet, for his words sustain and encourage the weary and draw our attention not only to Israel's sin and the servant's obedience, but the compassion of Christ. We not only hear and take heed to the prophet's words, but we know also that the word has been made flesh in Jesus Christ. The words of the prophet in this text can be words that Christ himself spoke as he faced his accusers and tormentors and as he prepared for his own death upon his entry into Jerusalem. Hear the words of the prophet which can be the words of Christ which sustain the weary in times of trial and difficulty.

"... I have not been rebellious and I have not drawn back." Lord, you know that I have kept your commandments and your word. You know that I have kept the faith and fought the good fight. I have not been detoured or distracted by my enemies. I have kept my eyes on your prize. I have not shirked my duties or shrunk from my tasks or allowed my detractors to destroy my purpose and intent. I have stood for truth. I have kept the faith. I have kept your word. Through it all I have not drawn back from the things you have required of me.

"I offered my back to those who beat me, my cheeks to those who pulled out my beard." Those who beat me tried to humiliate and dehumanize me, but I kept my back straight. I stood tall. I refused to trade evil with evil. I refused to submit to the reign of terror invoked against me. I did not bow down to the gods of violence, but gave my back as a cushion, as a foundation to those who beat me. They pulled out my beard and drew blood but I have

43

refused to draw the blood of my enemies. They beat me. They mocked me. They jeered me. They scorned me. They flayed my flesh with the lash. They pierced my flesh with their sharp weapons. They beat me down, but I stood tall with my back straight and my head high. They tried to desecrate me but only defiled themselves. They castigated my family and denounced my lineage and heritage and still I have stood for thee.

"I did not hide my face from mocking and spitting." Why should I hide my face? This is the face you gave me to look with compassion on my enemies. The face you gave me with eyes to convey comfort to those who are hurting and lost. I did not hide my face. Why should I hide my face from the faces of those whose mouths mock and spit at me and whose teeth are clenched? There is no shame in my face. There is no disgrace in my brow. There is no terror in my eyes. Why should I drop my head in humiliation? Why should I hide my eyes from thee? Why should I look towards the ground instead of the heavens whence I have been called to do your work? Why should I not look my enemies straight in their eyes? Why should I allow my eyes to show fear and trembling and sickness unto death? Why should I allow the ridicule, disdain, and arrogance of my enemies to cause me to look away from thee? I am your son. Your face is my face. I am made in your image.

I will not hide my face. Cowards hide their faces. The devil hides his face. Those who are less than honorable and righteous hide their faces to do evil. But I will not hide my face. It is the face of love, truth, and righteousness in the face of hatred, untruth, and unrighteousness. It is the face of triumph in the presence of defeat, the face of joy in the midst of terrible sorrow. I will not give my enemies the satisfaction that they have put fear in my heart by hiding my face. Let them spit in my face. Let them mock me to my face as I look through their eyes. I will not flinch. I will neither be ashamed nor embarrassed by what they have done!

"For I will not be disgraced ... and I know I will not be put to shame." My enemies do not disgrace me but themselves. My enemies do not put me to shame but shame themselves. Why should I be disgraced? Why should I be ashamed? Why should I view myself through the eyes of my enemies which have been shamed and disgraced by what they have done to me?

Why should I adopt the mindset and viewpoint of my enemies whose purpose is to desecrate and destroy what is God's? To view myself with shame and disgrace is to view myself as the perpetrator of crimes. It is to see myself as my enemy sees me and that is without love, mercy, or compassion. Why should I give my enemy the authority to determine and dictate how I shall see myself and how I shall see him? Why should I give my enemy this power over me? I shall never allow the mind of my enemy to become my mind so that I see both him and myself as he sees me. I shall never allow the spirit of my enemy to become my spirit.

Therefore, I have no disgrace and I have no shame because I see myself as you would see me, Father, through the eyes of grace, love, mercy, and truth. I have no shame. I am not disgraced, for the enemy shall not cause me to do to him and think of him as he does to me and thinks of me. I shall never give my enemy that kind of power, for when I do, I do as he does and think as he thinks, and only you, Father, have that power over my doing and thinking.

"Who then brings charges against me? Let us face each other. Who is my accuser? Let him confront me. Who is he who condemns me? They will all wear out like a garment." What then are the charges? What are the causes of these accusations and recriminations? What are the causes of all this beating and mocking and spitting? What then are the charges? What are the crimes? Loving and serving God's people? Calling the wicked into account? Exhorting the people back to God? Finding the lost? Feeding the hungry? Enriching the poor? Visiting the prisoners? Releasing the oppressed? Challenging the powers and principalities? Exhorting the people of God to grow and not become stagnant and still? Not shaking hands with the devil? Telling Satan to get behind me? Not selling out to the Romans, pagans, and Jews? Speaking the truth? Saving the unsaved? Restoring the dead and dying?

What then are the crimes? What are the charges? Building the church? Equipping the saints to serve in love? Casting out demons? Raising Lazarus? Not humiliating my enemies in the way they have tried to humiliate me? What are the charges? Helping the widows?

Loving the little children? A willingness to be crucified for the sins of the world? What are the charges? Healing on the sabbath? Sitting and eating with sinners? Having women to support my movement? Choosing the most unlikely to succeed as my disciples? Quitting my job as a carpenter and receiving the call of the Father to make fishers of men and women?

What are the charges? Calling women into ministry? Loving those who are gay and different? Refusing you the privilege of stoning a prostitute? Refusing to judge and condemn people to the point of repudiation and death? What are the charges? Paying taxes to Caesar? Feeding the 5,000? Giving you be-attitudes that will help you get better? Who are my accusers? What are the charges? They will all wear out like garments and the moths will eat them up.

Are you weary? Are you tired? Are you mocked? Are you scorned? Are you accused? Have your enemies spat at you, beaten you, and rejected you? God will sustain you with his word. God will deliver you through his love. God will give you triumph over all that you are facing, for it is the sovereign God who helps me, who comes to my aid in time of trouble and gives me victory over those who scorn and persecute me.

The word has become flesh in me and I will sustain you in all that you face. Come, ye who are weary, and be sustained with this word!

A Blood That Passes Over

Exodus 12:1-4, 5-10, 11-14

In our lesson the Lord gives precise instructions to Moses and Aaron on the content and preparation of the Passover meal. The blood of a lamb with no defects on the door frames of their houses would be the sign for God to pass over them and not strike them down with their Egyptian oppressors. The lamb would therefore be a sacrifice for the person who would have perished from the plague of God's wrath. The blood is a symbol of innocence, purity, and oblation to the Lord. This feast of Passover would continue as an annual holiday in honor of the night that the Lord passed over the homes of the Israelites and spared their lives. It would signify a time of preparation for the fulfillment of God's promises. It would also be a time of remembrance of how God delivered the Hebrews from the Egyptians and thus allowed them to escape the bitterness of slavery and haunting memories of formerly oppressed people.

Just as the blood of the innocent lamb was shed as a sacrifice and substitute for the sins and infirmities of the Israelite community, Christ today is our paschal lamb, our lamb of God, our unblemished savior who sacrificed his life for the salvation of souls and the remission of sins. Christ's blood is offered for the sins of all people. His blood passes over all of our past wrongs, infirmities, and imperfections. The perfect lamb is offered as a sacrifice for God's people, and it is his blood that serves as a source of redemption, power, hope, liberation, and love for the faith community. The holy lamb of God is offered as a sacrifice for the sins of the whole world. His blood is a symbol of redemption for a people enslaved by sin.

There are three primary realities that God "passed over" to redeem and save the Israelites from Egypt which have important implications in Christ's blood passing us from the sins of our present age.

The blood of the lamb passes over our condemnation as sinners. As coconspirators in our own enslavement, we have been judged to be eternally branded and condemned for our sins. It is not far-fetched to believe that many of the Israelites may have been conformed to their own captivity due to a lack of faith and the presence of fear. The sin of slavery is not only visited upon the enslavers for their terror and brutality but is imposed upon the enslaved who, through a lack of faith and trust in God, comply with their own bondage. There were those who committed sins and errors by consorting with their captors by acquiescing with a system of slavery and oppression that would bring long term condemnation for the oppressed. While the plague was inflicted upon the Egyptians for their role in the enslavement process, eternal condemnation and perpetual penalty hung over the heads of the Israelites for their lack of faith and for the disobedience that instigated their servitude. God could have easily allowed the judgment of eternal penalty and condemnation to reign, but instead God allowed the blood of the lamb to become a symbol of God's passing over their past errors and sins.

And so it is with Christ our lamb of God who passes over the sins of our disobedience, our own complicity with the slavery of sin. It is the blood of Christ that passes over our sin, that lifts the eternal condemnation and penalty of death that sin warrants and wages. It is the blood of Christ, our unblemished paschal lamb whose sacrifice and blood become the sources of atonement, or *at-one-ment*, with his people. The blood of Christ provides a way out of the eternal penalty reserved for the uncontrite and the unrepentant, who revel in the slavery of sin and bask in its after-effects. The blood of the lamb therefore passes over our eternal condemnation by spiritual exoneration.

The blood of the lamb passes over our persecution as sinners. God could have easily chosen to continue the persecution of Egypt. God could have easily continued his wrath of rage instead of showing grace and mercy. That God would allow the homes of the Israelites to be passed over is a sign of God's favor and love instead of his anger and ire. That God would send us his only son instead of perpetuating a much-deserved persecution is a sign of God's continuing favor and love.

The Israelites were persecuted by their captors and enemies. As Christians we are persecuted for and by our sins. The blood of Christ provides a way out of the persecution; a way of redemption and salvation amid the calamities of our condition. By allowing sin to take residency in our minds, hearts, and souls, and by giving sin legal rights, we give sin a dominion and providence which foments the conditions for our continued persecution and estrangement from God. We are persecuted by our sin. Our sin is a sign of our ongoing persecution by the adversaries of God. We pursue our own persecution through our acquiescence with sin. Our persecution can therefore become self-inflicted, self-generated, and self-perpetuated.

Christ our lamb of God was offered up as a way out of the persecution; a way out of the damnation, oppression, and subjugation that sin has created. Our lives no longer need sin's ratification or sponsorship, for we have been given a way out of the fury, ire, frenzy, and choler of sin's devastation. We no longer have to run to sin, take refuge in sin, live for sin, or die for sin. We no longer have to become spiritual refugees of a persecution that is eternal. There is a way out of sin and a way into Christ. The way into Christ is the way out of sin. It is a road less traveled; a road that leads in two directions with two destinations. No longer refugees of persecution, the blood of the lamb wipes clean the slate of persecution that sin engraves upon the human heart.

The Israelites no longer had to experience a persecution that came with their own condemnation and that of their enemies. Christians no longer have to experience eternal persecution due to the reign and terror of sin in their lives. Sin that is self-directed and

self-inflicted no longer warrants our living as the eternally persecuted, because the blood of the lamb wipes clean the ledger of sin.
This does not mean that we are no longer sinners. It only means
that the memory of the sin recorded in the collective conscious-
ness of the community and its individuals does not rationalize or
justify the continued persecution of the redeemed of God. It also
means that sin does not have ultimate dominion, hegemony, and
authority in our lives so as to domesticate our continued estrangement from God. This persecution cannot be warranted from self-
inflicted sins nor can it be justified by the sins others inflicted upon
us or those we inflict upon them. There is a way out. The blood of
the lamb passes over our eternal persecution and redeems us for
his glory by giving us an opportunity to begin anew in Christ.

Finally the blood of the lamb passes over our prosecution as
sinners. The judgment of condemnation leads to persecution and
prosecution for our sins. Prosecution leads to execution and death.
Without Christ and the blood that passes over we are eternally
doomed to die unredeemed deaths from the wages of our sins. The
Israelites could not be prosecuted in the courts of Egypt because
the blood of the lamb had caused God to pass them over. Now they
would not undergo a death sentence. Now they would not be en-
shrouded in a great cloud of unknowing. They knew God had forgiven them. They knew that the sentence had been stayed and ac-
quittal had come. No longer would the jury be out. No longer would
the jury be hung. No longer would their progress towards freedom
be overshadowed by their liberation from Egypt. God's eternal law
prevailed over man's tyrannical law. Divine law and judgment
would supersede and eclipse man's judgment and pronouncements
of death. They would no longer be prosecuted by their enemies
because the blood of the lamb, the sacrifice of the lamb, has wiped
clean the ledger of death.

And so it is with Christ. No longer need we be prosecuted in
the eternal courts of damnation and judgment. No longer must we
be subject to the humiliation of arrest, incarceration, and punish-
ment in the courts of evil.

If the devil is our adversary, Christ is our ally and mighty
counselor. If evil is our antagonist, Christ is our protagonist. If

prosecution is our sentencer, salvation is our supreme court of appeal. The ban has been lifted. The judgment has been rendered "not guilty" by reason of the blood. "Not guilty" by reason of repentance, redemption, and remission of sin. The blood has passed over our eternal prosecution in the courts of Belial and Beelzebub.

It is a blood that passes over our condemnation, persecution, and prosecution as sinners, for a comforter has come, a counselor has come to show us a way out of sin and a way into salvation. God passes over our blame, our affliction, our pestilence, our iniquity, and our pain through his innocent and sacrificial blood. "I know it was the blood." I know it is the blood that saves, redeems, and renews poor sinners. It is a blood that is simple. A blood that is pure. A blood that is righteous. A blood that seals and saves those who seek him. Thank God for a blood that passes over past mistakes and gives us an opportunity to unite with Christ in covenant against the prospects and memory of our oppression as God's people!

Good Friday

Deformed, Disfigured, And Despised: A Marred But Magnificent Messiah

Isaiah 52:13—53:12

The prophet gives the report, but who will believe it? The servant will act wisely. He will be lifted up and exalted. The problem is the new Messiah does not fit the description of the Holy One of Israel, the gallant one, the defiant and courageous who shall lift God's people out of the dregs of despair. He shall not come as one standing upright, but one who is disfigured and deformed, despised and rejected; a man of sorrows acquainted with grief. Who would believe such a report? That God would choose a lowly, humble servant upon whose shoulders the government would rest and who would be called the wonderful counselor?

Isaiah's depiction of the new Messiah does not meet the customary profile of success. He is the most unlikely to succeed. There is no beauty or majesty to attract us to him. He is familiar with suffering and will take upon himself our infirmities and our sorrows as the stricken of God. Could this be a travesty, a comedy of error? Could this be some kind of charade? How could the Messiah be deformed and disfigured, despised and rejected? How could this new Messiah usher in the new age with power and authority when he himself is so lowly and broken? How could it be that God would choose and call such an unlikely person to have such power and authority amid raging powers and principalities?

How could he heal others when he could not heal himself? How could he save others when he could not save himself? How could he bring hope and joy and the promise of the new Jerusalem with so sad a countenance, with so disfigured a body, with such a marred appearance? The image in Isaiah contradicts the image of

53

the brave, stalwart warrior riding into Jerusalem on a white horse, brandishing swords and daggers to herald the violent overthrow of the enemies of God. This image of Isaiah is both poignant and deeply disturbing. God is using a new formula of the suffering servant to bring a new hope to new generations.

Josephus corroborates Isaiah's description of the Messiah in his book *Halosis*. The redactive and reconstructive work of Robert Eisler in the *Messiah Jesus and John the Baptist* confirms Jesus as a man of sorrows acquainted with grief. He is not attractive. "He is dark skinned, hunchbacked, with a long face and a long nose, with eyebrows above the nose so that spectators can take fright. He is a short man. He is an ugly man." This image of Jesus is not pretty. He is not someone who attracts the multitudes who are able and well, but compels those who are disfigured and marred like him to come unto him. Hear the words echoed in the temple that day, "Physician, heal thyself." The first century Jesus does not resemble the beautiful, attractive Jesus depicted today in modern art. He was something other; wholly different than what we see today. He was hideous. So horrible was he that we would hide our faces from him in disbelief.

The blind, lame, and lepers, the disfigured, despised, and marred came to him to receive healing from him. Yet he could not heal himself. Jesus attracted these people unto him. Why? Was there something about his physical condition that enabled them to identify with him? Because he looked like them did they sense he could provide a cure for them? Jesus embodies two basic contradictory realities: one of being deformed, disfigured, and despised, which is the man we shall never want to be; and the other is having the power to heal others, which is the man we hope to become. He at once is the personification of the extremities of our human condition. He is the man we never want to become and the man we want to become. Being disfigured and marred, he was utterly unattractive, which means his looks were repelling, repugnant, and repulsive. On the other hand, having this healing and redeeming power, he was compelling, attractive, and embraceable. Two powers on the opposite ends of the human and spiritual spectrum. One is the power to repel others away defensively. The other is the power to attract others to him offensively. This is the cross.

The new Messiah would become a perfect physical representation of our lowest and basest condition as humanity. He would also become the epitome of a perfect spiritual representation of our highest humanity. He is at once the man we never want to be seen with, never want to be around, never want in our company, but also the man we long for, the man whose company we seek, the one whose presence and power uplifts and enhances our reality as human persons.

He was deformed, says Eisler, due to a spinal kyphosis, which was not an uncommon malady developed by artisans of his time. There is speculation that Paul may have suffered from the same condition. He was disfigured; there was no beauty in his spinal curvature and marred appearance.

He was despised because few people understood how these extremities of rejection and attraction, of magnificent power and utter powerlessness, of exaltation and humility, could be combined into a single body. What was more offensive was the fact that he couldn't or didn't even heal himself. He had the power to heal others but wouldn't heal himself. He had the power to raise and heal others but wouldn't exalt himself. He had the power to transform and save lives, yet he couldn't save himself. What a paradox! What a contradiction!

He would not save himself, but he would save others by dying on a cross and rising from a grave. Here was a man who rebuffed, disgusted, and even nauseated people by his very presence. Yet he would conquer the forces of evil and death by dying on a cross and rising from the grave. To add insult to injury, he would give the same power to his followers and those who believed and had faith in him. Who would believe this insane report? Where crooked roads are made straight and rough places plain, where high places would be brought low and low places high? The paradox of this contradiction is a riddle; a great enigma.

The Messiah should be someone we should look up to. (So they thought.) Someone bold, fearless and attractive. Someone handsome, pretty, and wholesome. He would be violent. Someone who would destroy our enemies and make them his footstool. He would use hatred and divisiveness among the people as a weapon of conquest. Someone we would want to cuddle and embrace but who would put a permanent hurt on our enemies. The new Messiah would usher in the new age and all would bow at his feet and be subject to his dominion and authority.

How could our conquering hero be a suffering servant? Could this little, scrawny hunch-backed man become our savior for the ages? Why would God play such a cruel trick upon his people? He is ugly and unattractive. He cannot save himself. He has no political connections. He has no money in the bank and no armies marching behind him by day and by night. He has no large following. His disciples are a rag-tag bunch. He quit his job as a carpenter. He is homeless and jobless. He is friendless and wifeless. He has no children or posterity to carry on his name. He walks everywhere he goes. He is not a citizen of Rome or a rabbi in the best of our traditions. He goes to banquets with sinners. He attracts the blind, lame, deaf, and dumb. He heals the sick. He casts out demons. He raises the dead. He owns no weapons and he is an outcast of the Roman and Jewish establishments. Could this deformed, disfigured, and despised person be the new Messiah?

Being deformed he took on our deformities, our afflictions, and our grief. Being disfigured, he took on our unattractiveness, the horror of our disbelief. Being despised he took on our condition as outcasts and spiritual pariahs, as means of our relief.

He was a marred but magnificent Messiah. We don't want to see him, but we want to touch him. We don't want to suffer with him but want him to be our suffering servant. We don't want his physical looks but want his spiritual power. We don't want his association but want to claim his authority.

He was marred for our sins, iniquities, afflictions, and addictions. He was magnificent in the way that he bore our sorrows and took on our condition and freed us from enslavement to that condition. He was marred by our scars. We killed him! But by his scars and stripes we are healed. He was marred as the lowly and rejected of God. He was magnificent in the way that he raised us from the dregs and doldrums of sin and despair making us the accepted of

God. He was marred in his grief but magnificent in the way he triumphed over suffering and the dirty things we did to him. He came to us to save us, and we killed him. But he got up from the grave and still comes to us with a message of love and redemption!

We pay tribute today to this Messiah — this most unlikely to succeed; this man of sorrows acquainted with grief; this one who had no beauty in which to behold him, but who had more love, power, compassion, and strength than any man who has walked this earth. We pay tribute to him as a marred man without the earthly amenities, but also as a magnificent man with all heavenly power and authority. We pay tribute to him as one who was despised and rejected, but also as a man who stood as our accepted of God in the hour of great need.

He was marred but he was magnificent. He was lowly but exalted. He was rejected but accepted. He was disfigured but reconfigured the parameters of eternity. He was not attractive to look upon, but he loved us so much that he gave his life for us to make us attractive in the eyes of God and all creation.

All praises due to the deformed, disfigured, and rejected one who stood in our place against the power of evil and gave us victory! If we might come anywhere close to his shining example of manhood and exemplify his holy boldness and strength of character, God the Father would be pleased.

The savior of the world was not someone whose beauty we looked to but someone whose power we looked up to. He was not a man who could be measured by the superficial indices of this world, because he came to save the world. We pay tribute to Jesus, a marred but magnificent Messiah who gave his life for his people that they might become the man that he was and have the love, power, and joy that he shared through the gift of salvation!

He Commanded Us To Preach

Acts 10:34-43

Opposition to preaching the risen Christ and reaching the Gentiles emerged early in the ministry of the apostles. Peter and the others quickly found themselves on the front lines of defense against attacks regarding the cogency and credibility of the message they were preaching. Emboldened by the presence and power of the Holy Ghost, many of the apostles gained renewed fortitude in proclaiming the message of Christ to Jewish and Gentile communities in the early days of the church.

Anytime the gospel is preached with authority and power invariably there will be those who line up in opposition to the message. These forces of blistering belligerence often question the authenticity of the message, if not the credentials and authority of the messengers. Peter reminded his audience that Christ "commanded us to preach!" In other words, there is no shirking and compromise with those powers and principalities that seek to neutralize the impetus of the message and efficacy of the messenger. Christ issued the command that the word should go forth with power and authority so as to make new disciples of all nations.

The problem in Peter's time were those enemies outside of the early faith community who aligned themselves in opposition to the message of the followers of the way. Today, much opposition comes from those within the faith community who have so distanced themselves from the word of God that it appears as foreign dogma when preached to sore and itching ears. They do not want to hear the truth. They simply want to be placated, appeased, and soothed.

They never want their sin called out nor do they want to be afflicted out of their spiritual safe houses.

The problem today is both preachers who have compromised, sanitized, and dethorned the gospel in order to appease certain people within the church, as well as people in the church who don't want to hear the word of God preached with power and authority because of sin and self-complacency.

The truth of the matter is God help the preacher who does not preach and God help the church who does not want the pure, unadulterated gospel to be preached to the living and the dead!

There is a story of a young preacher who was asked to leave his pastorate by parishioners because his preaching was too "Bible oriented." His predecessor had preached out of newspapers, sailing manuals, and other instruction booklets, but seldom used the Bible as a text for preaching. When he began his ministry by teaching and preaching from the Bible, the people were appalled and outraged because he used texts that both comforted and afflicted them. They were not accustomed to sound biblical preaching and many of them rose up in protest. Can you imagine this sad picture of a church rebuking a young pastor because they do not want to hear preaching that is biblically based? The problem of such contempt for preaching is not uncommon in some churches and denominations.

There are numerous stories in Christendom of men and women called by God to use their gifts to preach God's word, who have been intimidated by parishioners to tone down the power and authority of their preaching. In the case of Peter, he is exhorting the truth about Christ crucified and Christ resurrected. His commission to his disciples is to preach and teach under the anointing of the Holy Ghost! But Peter reminds his hearers that God commanded us to preach!

Paul exhorts Timothy in his second letter, "Preach the Word; be prepared in season and out of season; correct, rebuke and encourage with great patience and careful instruction. For the time will come when people will not put up with sound doctrine (2 Timothy 4:2-3a).

Paul also says in Romans 10:14-15, "How, then can they call on the one they have not believed in? And how can they believe in the one of whom they have not heard? And how can they hear without someone preaching to them? And how can they preach unless they are sent?"

Peter affirms a central task of the Christian church and its leaders to preserve and preach the gospel for all generations and times. In his time the challenge was to preach the Good News to the Jews and Gentiles. In our time we must preach the Good News to the Jews, the Gentiles, and those who are in the church. For being in the church, many have grown weary of hearing and are in need of a conversion or reconversion experience to Christ.

He commanded us to the gospel of peace. The Good News of peace is still needed in our time. In a world that is still torn by war, bloodshed, and strife, the message of peace and goodwill should go forth for all time. Nations are not only at war with each other, but children and youth are at war with their parents, the young are at war with the old, good is at war with evil. Poor and rich, black and white are engaged in an endless struggle for freedom, power, and autonomy. The world is one large P.O.W. camp.

There is a physical war being waged for people's lives. There is a spiritual war being waged for people's souls. Everywhere we look in society we see the awful specter of warfare. Young people carry guns to schools and murder their classmates in cold blood and then kill themselves. People have no shame today. Grown men go into churches and synagogues to kill the innocent children and youth. There is the war on poverty and the war on drugs. There is a cultural war being waged for the hearts and souls of the young people of this nation, where the music they listen to and the movies they watch desensitize them to the need for self-respect and respect for others. Everywhere we look we see the devastation and fallout of spiritual and physical warfare.

The resurgence of hate groups and the erosion of certain individual rights creates a seething cauldron of violence, trepidation, and hatred in our society. The gospel of peace needs to be preached more than ever today.

It is a gospel that respects all people and affirms all people regardless of sex, sexual orientation, age, ethnicity, or race. It is a

61

gospel that seeks to understand personal pain and the pain of others and accordingly seeks to reconcile differences. It is a gospel that seeks forgiveness and redemption for our brothers and sisters. We need the gospel of peace preached more than ever today in a world that is living by the sword and dying by the sword.

He commanded us to preach the gospel of truth. Why are people afraid of the truth? Is it because we punish and kill our truth tellers and reward our liars with accolades and praise? Why are people afraid to love one another as Christ has loved them? Why have so many of us been cast under the spell of untruthfulness and disdain or dislike for another because he or she is different?

One of the great tragedies of the modern church is the manner in which the gospel of truth has been compromised and neutralized by the messengers of Christ. People are afraid of the truth. They are afraid to look at themselves and see themselves truthfully. But Jesus says, "You shall know the truth and the truth shall set you free."

Preachers are afraid to speak the truth to their own churches and society at large for fear of losing their jobs or status in their communities. Have we become so establishment-oriented that we cannot speak the truth and love in ways that will set the church free from its present sins? Truth tellers are called whistle blowers. Many of them have been ostracized and stigmatized by their own families and communities.

Some churches have become bastions and citadels of untruth. The power of the gospel has been liquidated by a prevailing atmosphere of lies and untruths that have become a part of church life and culture. Preachers are afraid to confront people creatively and lovingly for wrongdoing and are afraid to put themselves on trial for their own sins. Parishioners are afraid to confront preachers and other parishioners for fear of rejection and rebuke. What emerges, then, is a culture of lies, untruths, and deception that is promulgated under the guise of not wanting to hurt the other guy's feelings. But if we approach people in love and with the awareness that we are all sinners in need of God's amazing grace, why can't we speak the truth in and outside of the church in love? Ephesians 4:15 promotes "speaking the truth in love."

Do we fear to speak the truth because we are afraid of the wrath and pain that will fall on our heads for truth telling? Is it because we fear crucifixion and repudiation by our fellows and thus we avoid being messengers of truth altogether? In what ways do we compromise the mission and ministry of the church by not being truthful with ourselves and the people we are called to love and serve? Are we hiding in our churches from truth? Are we afraid to preach the gospel on Sundays because we fear the "ouch" more than we want the "amen"? The church could not be the church without those who were willing to tell the truth that we might be free from the bondage of sin and death. *Christ has commanded us to preach gospel truth to set ourselves and the people free from the constraints that prevent them from having life fully.*

He commanded us to preach the gospel of love. What the world needs today is unselfish, agape love. What the world needs today is caring and redemptive love. We hear the gospel of hate touted by hate groups. We hear the language of contempt and strife hurled at our fellows — menacing words, excoriating words, words that maul and hurt, afflict and convict.

Love is still the most powerful force in the world. Love is a spiritual elixir; a divine diuretic that rids us of the excesses that prevent us from complete fellowship with our neighbors.

The gospel is a message of love for all people and not just some people. That gospel of love should be preached and taught with unwavering fire and unwaning enthusiasm. Christ commanded us to preach his gospel of love!

He commanded us to preach the gospel of repentance and forgiveness. We all need to repent of something and be forgiven of something. We all need to learn to forgive ourselves and forgive others of wrongdoing. Christ forgives us of our sins and we are to forgive others. But there should also be repentance, a turning away from sin and a turning towards remorse and conviction to make ourselves and others better.

We cannot therefore compromise the gospel of Christ's crucifixion and resurrection, for he commanded us to preach. Our great commission may be found in Luke 4:18-19 as well as Matthew 28:19-20:

"The Spirit of the Lord is on me because he has anointed me to preach the good news to the poor. He has sent me to proclaim freedom for the prisoners and recovery of sight for the blind, to release the oppressed, to proclaim the year of the Lord's favor."

We must preach that Christ died and that Christ was resurrected, which means that the old man in us must die so that the new man can be born again. We must therefore preach repentance and forgiveness. For it is a gospel of reconciliation. This reconciliation is extended to the poor and the oppressed, which proclaims and affirms the year of the Lord's favor.

We must preach repentance and forgiveness, a gospel of love and reconciliation. How much more worse off would the world be without a message of repentance, reconciliation, and redemption? How much more sorrow would we endure? How much more trouble could we take without hope of ever being reconciled to our enemies and detractors and those we have hurt through our sins of omission and commission? The gospel provides a way to harmonize and neutralize the chaos of our lives. It gives us a way of saying, "I am sorry," to our brothers and sisters. It helps us to start all over. We must never cease preaching the gospel of repentance and forgiveness, for we are all in great need of this great mercy of God.

Finally, we must preach a gospel of liberation and freedom. People should be set free from sin, the burdens of past wrongs and mistakes and the things other people have done to them, and the baggage of anger, remorse, betrayal, frustration, and confusion. People need to be set free from hopelessness, unrighteousness, non-forgiveness, and vengeance.

Christ came to set people free from all forms of bondage that keep them from actualizing potential and receiving salvation in order to live wholesome, productive, and spirit-filled lives. We have too much baggage, too much anger, too many painful memories of the past that dash our hope for the future. Too many things bind us and choke off the life of the spirit in us. We need to be set free from our sins of me-ism, racism, sexism, ageism, and other isms that bind and destroy our sense of community. Parents carry emotional, spiritual, and psychological baggage and pass that baggage on to their children who pass it on to their children. The spiral of iniquity spins out of control from generation to generation. People need to be set free from the various forms of psychological, emotional, spiritual, and social bondage that kill the spirit of God in them and cause them to turn against their brothers and sisters.

The addictions, afflictions, and pestilence that cause us to be in bondage need to be challenged. Preaching a gospel of liberation and freedom will set people free from the various hindrances and encumbrances that cause them to be spiritual exiles from God.

He commanded us to preach the word in season and out of season. Come hell or high water we must preach. The desire is like fire shut up in my bones. We must preach the word with power, authority, joy, and goodness as Peter and the apostles preached in the days of old. God give us the strength to preach the gospel unfettered and unfazed by the constraints and impediments that hinder the word from reaching present and future generations! God give us strength to preach the word with fire, compassion, joy, and praise. That God commanded us to preach a gospel of truth, love, reconciliation and forgiveness, and freedom and liberation is a task that we should forever cherish. God commanded us to preach! Let us do it in ways that will bring honor to the saints and glory to God always!

Obeying God Rather Than Men

Acts 5:27-32

How many times have we borne witness to this scene? Men and women of the Gospel attacked by their enemies for preaching the resurrected Christ? How many times have we seen this inevitable and inimitable skirmish between the horizontal and the vertical, the spiritual and the carnal, the things of man and the things of God? How many times have we seen this scene within and without the church, where servants of the Lord who have confessed with their mouths that Jesus is Lord and believe in their hearts that God raised him from the dead are confronted by those of the unsaved who want to give strict orders to "keep your mouth shut and not teach in his name"?

Here Peter and the apostles are confronted by the Sanhedrin and the high priest who issue this audacious command, which in reality was a threat to keep silent. The high priest, his henchmen, and their Roman overseers would later gang up on the apostles to scare them into shutting their mouths about the risen Christ.

"How can you talk about a Christ that is risen when we just killed him? He is dead! He is dead! He is dead! We killed him and we will kill you if you don't keep your mouth shut! How dare you speak about a man that we have silenced, that we have put to shame; a man that we hung on the cross and saw take his last breath? How dare you talk of a man whom we humiliated, crowned with thorns, made carry his own cross, pierced his side, stole his garments, and made a public disgrace? How dare you stand before us, Peter, and tell us that this same man is risen? That this same man whom we saw laid in the grave is now alive and living? What is this Peter?

67

To say that he is risen to us is an act of treasonous revenge. How can you say that a man that we are responsible for killing now lives? Is this some kind of threat? Are you mocking the powers that be? For if you say he is risen, we take this to mean that he is coming back for those of us who were responsible for killing him! Your resurrection pronouncements are really, Peter, not innocent spiritual verbiage, but a declaration of war on the enemies of Christ! We command you to shut your mouth! We are giving you strict orders to keep your mouth shut! We do not want to hear anymore of this man's teachings!"

How familiar are these words to those who proclaim his resurrection? The enemies of Christ issue their threats for the servants and saints of God to keep their mouths shut. For to talk of resurrection is to speak with a freedom that man did not originate. This kind of power can only come from God, for man has the power to kill but does not have the power to resurrect those who have been killed in his name.

We see this familiar scenario time and again, where the devil and the enemies of Christ issue threats to his servants to keep their mouths shut under the strictest orders. The caveat is really a veiled death threat.

I have seen it even in the church where servants of the gospel are threatened by powers and principalities in the church, admonished and warned to do things man's way and not God's way. This confrontation between man's way and God's way is the continuing conflict in the church and is the axis of the power struggle of darkness and light.

Some people want to run the church man's way rather than serve the church God's way. Man's way says we don't talk about the Holy Ghost because he has gone out of style. We don't believe in basic Bible study because it is too fundamental. We don't emphasize all of the gifts of the Holy Spirit because we think only certain types of gifts are acceptable. The "strict orders" create a perpetual confrontation between people who say "what we do and don't do" rather than ask "what God wants us to do."

One preacher lamented the tough time he had in challenging his congregation to tithe. Rather than many of them admitting they didn't want to tithe, they challenged his authority and became irate at his using Scriptures to corroborate the mandates to tithe. They had become so used to doing things their way they did not even acknowledge God's way as the right way.

I recall in my own experience the struggle in implementing a hymn of invitation after the proclamation. The church did not even invite people to Christ after the word was preached. There were several people who became very angry and disgruntled that I would even open the doors of the church after the sermon. They had been so used to doing things their way rather than God's way they nearly went into open rebellion.

I have heard the story of one preacher being confronted by parishioners because the gospel was preached on sin, fornication, adultery, and theft. One preacher said that a committee was formed to oust him from his pastorate because he preached a sermon series on the seven deadly sins. "We are not used to hearing those kinds of sermons and we would rather you preach on love and forgiveness than on sin. We don't want to hear any of your damnation sermons."

What nerve! What audacity to have the gall to tell the preacher what to preach! I have heard of laity who have been confronted by other laity because they were being "too holy," or "too biblical" or "too spiritual." Some churches have become so accustomed to doing things man's way that they are completely subversive of God's way.

There are always forces that seek to compromise the power and efficacy of the gospel. There are always forces that seek to negate and prevent the gospel of truth being preached in full measure. The devil always gives strict orders on God's truth so that truth which ultimately disarms him and puts him on the run cannot go forth. There are always oppositional forces that are threatened by the gospel of Christ. They are threatened by a message of liberation and freedom, threatened by reconciliation and forgiveness, or threatened by the word of faith and truth. These forces are especially threatened because the gospel compels critical self-evaluation, and many of us are not willing to look squarely at ourselves.

The history of Christianity is replete with those saints of old who were willing to stand and proclaim the truth boldly and outrightly. They could not be silenced by the opposition. They refused to be cast under the spell of silence when God's truth needed to go forth. We can see Peter and the apostles standing against the Sanhedrin and the high priest proclaiming Christ crucified and Christ risen! We can see the early Christians standing before the emperors of Rome refusing to recant their allegiance to Christ and suffering martyrdom and death for their bravery and faith. We can see Martin Luther saying, "Here I stand," before the Catholic Church, refusing to compromise his basic faith and challenging its corruptions. We can see Dietrich Bonhoeffer sitting in his jail cell saying, "No," to Nazi tyranny and saying, "When Christ calls a man, he bids him come and die."

We can see the countless men and women, known and unknown, who have stood on hallowed ground and said, "No" to evil and "No" to those men and powers who wanted to mute their allegiance to Christ with their veiled threats of terror and death. We can see them in the church of Liebzig, the church of Russia and the other communist societies that threatened death for being Christian.

The apostle Paul in his letter to the Galatians proclaims in chapter one, verse ten, "Am I now trying to win the approval of men, or of God? Or am I trying to please men? If I were still trying to please men, I would not be a servant of Christ."

We are called to serve God and man, but a time may come when we must choose between them. Will we side with those who want us to give up the fundamental tenets and power of our faith? Will we side with men when it means persecuting and destroying others in the name of religious belief?

Will we side with men or God when it comes to doing what is right, moral, and just? Are we willing to stand for the truth, die for the truth, and do what God has called us to do, or will we sit in sniveling silence? Will we compromise and sell out our faith? Will we side with those who are wrong because we fear for our own lives? Will we keep our mouths shut under strict orders because we have been told to do so?

Will we keep our mouths shut under strict orders in face of corruption, our own sin, discrimination, persecution, annihilation, destruction, famine, pestilence, iniquity, drought, hunger, disease, racism, poverty, hatred, psychological and sexual abuse, sexism, ageism, classism, genocide, homicide, fratricide, and suicide? Will we keep our mouths shut under strict orders about a risen Christ who lives in the present age? The same Christ who was raised from the dead who walked on water and healed the sick?

Shall we keep silent about the Christ who can raise us from our graves of doubt, hopelessness, faithlessness, and despair? Shall we keep silent in the face of those forces of opposition that still seek to mute and kill his spirit that lives within us? The same forces that killed him were defeated by his resurrection. Those same forces of cynicism, evil, and terrorism seek to kill him today through our forced silence about what he has done in our lives.

Are you complying with the strict orders to keep your mouth shut about the risen Christ, or are you proclaiming his resurrection in the fullness of his glory? Are you obeying man or are you obeying God? Have you given up, or are you standing up for the one who has stood up and given his life for you and continues to give us life even now? Are you keeping your mouth shut under strict orders, or are you standing and proclaiming the truth in Christ's name?

Blind Man's Bluff?

Acts 9:1-6 (7-20)

Who would believe it? Saul, the primary punk adversary of the followers of the way, blind in Damascus? Saul, the instigator of Stephen's stoning and death, the one who breathed out murderous threats against the followers of Jesus, now in Damascus in a spiritual safe house? Is this a bluff? Could this be a trick? Could this be a game concocted by the enemies of Jesus to lure us into a trap? How could a man who was feared by so many now be a blind, helpless squatter at a house on a street called Straight?

Doubt, concern, anxiety, and trepidation came with the news. This man named Saul caused terror in the hearts of Jesus' people. He would spare no mercy. He held the coats of the gang who stoned Stephen. He would bark to them instructions during the killing. He was a criminal; a gangster of the first order; a heel who unleashed his dogs of prey with mercenary madness.

Moreover, he would hurt, maim, and jail believers. He would write letters, set bounties, and dispatch mob garrisons to arrest and kill them. He left no stone unturned and no avenue unexplored to strike unholy terror and fear in the minds of the followers, to prevent this rag-tag group of believers from spreading the Good News about a man named Jesus. "All this talk about Saul being blind is just another ploy, a gambit, to lure us into a dark place to have us killed. Any talk about Saul being converted is just a blind man's bluff to entice us and seduce us into wholesale slaughter. Is it true? Can we believe this report? Is Saul really blind or is this a bluff?"

It has to be true for we have heard there was an encounter on the Damascus Road that resulted in his blindness.

All reports indicate that after breathing out murderous threats against the followers of Jesus and after planning to lay traps for them in Damascus, Saul was knocked off his high horse on the Damascus Road. Nothing could stop this man from his persecution. Nothing would deter him from annihilating the followers of Jesus. But as he was traveling to Damascus, he met up with Jesus who asked him why he was persecuting his followers. He met a man greater than himself. He had a close encounter of the first kind that knocked him down to the ground. Jesus knew that of the gang of men who went with Saul to kill Christians, he had to waylay the head gangster. Jesus had to get the attention of the others, and he did this by waylaying the baddest and toughest of the lot.

So it is true. This man Saul was waylaid on the Damascus Road, knocked to the canvas, given a standing eight count, got up and was led into Damascus without sight. He had to be led like a baby. His men were astonished, confused, and thunderstruck. Saul had been struck down to the ground. His men were numb from the encounter and feared for their lives. Now the tables were turned. The persecutors were the persecuted. The routers were the routed. The hounders were the hounded. The gangsters were being gangstered. Only a force and power of the magnitude of Christ Jesus could turn him around and convert him into a new being for Christ. The waylaying was real. His blindness was not a bluff. Those who persecute the followers of Christ will experience a spiritual ambush, a major apocalyptic, cataclysmic upheaval that will knock them from their high horse and re-order their steps for Jesus.

Second, we have heard that he was taken to the house of Judas on a street called Straight.

He was not taken to Jump Street. He wasn't taken to Front Street. The report is he was taken to a house on Straight Street so he could have time to think about his ways and get straight with God. Saul had plenty of time to think about what he did and how he did it to the followers of the Way. So long as he had eyes he could see what he was doing, plan what he was doing, look into the eyes of his men who did the doing. So long as he had eyes he could survey the land, take note of the hideouts of the frightened followers, and have command of his prey as an eagle in flight.

Stern eyes. Haughty eyes. Patronizing and condescending eyes. Disdainful eyes. Eyes with no mercy and compassion. Eyes that had no tears nor tenderness; cold, relenting, bloodthirsty eyes were the eyes of Saul.

As a man who relied heavily on his eyes to plan and execute his premeditated murder of Christians, he would now be without the very sight that enabled him to do evil. As a man who used his keen vision and insight to anticipate and set traps for the followers, his eyes were indispensable to his crimes.

But now that sight was gone. Now he couldn't see where he was, know where he was going, or know how he would get there. Now he was blind and helpless without the evil sight that caused him to wreak havoc among believers. Now he was like mother justice, blindfolded, but without the scales of truth balancing in the sway of his mind and hands. Now he was blindfolded and could not see. The wicked sight taken away would be restored by a more glorious sight of the presence and power of Christ. Before he had evil eyes, now he would see through the eyes of Christ. "Saul, Saul, why do you persecute me?"

Now he was in a safe house on a street called Straight. Now the three days without sight, food, and water would straighten him out for the Lord's work. Now his crooked ways would be made straight. His rough edges would be made plain. His high and haughty ways would be brought low and made straight. He was in a safe house on Straight Street so the Lord could get him straight.

"Saul, do you know who I am? I am the one who formed you in your mother's womb. I am the one who put food on your table and clothes on your back. I am the one who gave you an education. I am the one who raised you up in a prosperous family. I am the one who commissioned you as a tent maker and gave you the health to make a living despite your thorn. I am the one who gifted your mind and loved you through the rough and tough times of your life. I am the one who helped your mother when she was sick. I am the one who gave you everything you have. So why, why, why do you persecute me?"

The three days of blindness on a street called Straight would forever transform his sight and insight so that he could see Jesus. If

Jesus were going to use him, Saul had to see Jesus for himself. During the three days of blindness in the house of Judas, he gained more sight and insight than he had in a lifetime. He would see more of God in his physical blindness than he would in a lifetime of 20/20 vision.

Here he could look retrospectively to see the error of his ways, introspectively to search his own mind and spirit, and prospectively into the future to see how Christ had planned to use him. The house of Judas on the street called Straight is the place where Saul has been taken to get right with Jesus so that Jesus could straighten him out to use him for kingdom building. That he is on a street called Straight is not a bluff. It is not a rumor. It is not a trick or a trap. He is really in a place where Christ has his crooked ways straight in order to help rather than persecute the followers of the way.

Third, we have heard that there has been a laying on of hands by a man named Ananias and his sight has been restored. Ananias, reluctant himself at first to believe that Saul could be so helpless, was told by God to lay hands on Saul so the Lord could use him for his glory. Filled with the Holy Ghost, Ananias anointed Saul, and immediately the scales fell off his eyes and his sight was restored. This man Saul was baptized, and fed to make strong, and now he is a new man named Paul who is a chief missionary for Christ. The laying on of hands was the icing on the cake. The laying on of hands was the final straw that restored his sight. The laying on of hands through the power and anointing of the Holy Ghost is what finally convinced Saul of the power of Christ.

He was blinded, yes. But he may have thought it was some kind of freak accident. He was lead on to a street called Straight and was without sight, food, and water for three days. He may have still thought that this experience was just an anomaly, an aberration of some kind. But what really convinced him was the powerful prayer of Ananias, the anointing of the Holy Ghost, and the feeling of regaining fully restored sight. So the report is true. It is not a bluff. The blind man has had his sight restored and is a new creature for Christ. No longer a persecutor of followers and an ally of the devil, he is now an advocate for the followers and an enemy of the adversary. For it is Christ Jesus who confronted him, challenged him, and converted him. It is only through the power of Christ that we can have our sight taken and restored. It is only through the power of Christ that we can be led to a safe house by strangers to be prayed for and have hands laid upon us to change our lives forever.

The man who was once blind does now see. He was blinded by darkness but now sees the light of Christ. He was blinded by his own envy, hatred, and ignorance, and now he sees what the power of love, mercy, forgiveness, and grace can do. It is not blind man's bluff where he tags those with sight with his blind fold still on. Nor is it blind man's bluff where he is pretending to be blind and still can see. He is now truly a new man in Christ who will be used for helping the saints and building God's kingdom rather than hurting the saints and destroying the works of Christ.

The encounter on the road to Damascus, a street called Straight, and the laying on of hands has convinced us that the conversion of Saul was not a bluff or a game. For Christ truly came and changed his life and will change ours too on the roads of life. All things Christ can make new. His love, mercy, and power can change us from a life of persecution to a life of joy and service. No one can call God's bluff. It is Christ who calls us, saves us, anoints us, and equips us for service to his people. Christ will open our eyes and allow us to see what he sees just as he did to Saul on the Damascus Road.

A Sense Of Urgency

Acts 9:36-43

In the world we appear to be in a hurry to go nowhere and be on time. In the church we sometimes appear to be going in myriad directions in slow motion and with no sense of urgency. There are some things in life that require our immediate and exigent attention, and it is important that we are on time in the things of God. God is always on time with us. There is an adage in the African American community that church folks use often. "He may not always come when we call him, but he is always on time." In other words, God tends to our needs quickly and urgently. All situations require a 911 response. Are we on time and in time in the things of God and the church?

In hearing of Tabitha's death, Peter went immediately with the disciples to tend to her needs. He did not waste time. He did not consult his date book to see if he could squeeze the time in to see about the dead woman. He could have reasoned that since she was dead, it was too late to respond urgently. He could have placed it as last on his long list of other priorities. He could have taken his own sweet time to get there. Instead he went immediately with the disciples because the matter was of utmost importance.

Arriving at the home of the dead woman, he prayed for her, laid hands on her, and restored her to life. The power of his miracle was glorious, but the timing of his miracle was even more important because timing is sometimes everything.

I remember years ago while I was away in college, I had an aunt dying of cancer in Montreal, Canada. I kept putting off my letter of love and encouragement to her. After finally getting around to writing the letter, I later learned that it had arrived a day after she died. Had I taken the time to make this matter a priority, she could have received that letter in plenty of time. I was too late. Timing is important. Timing is everything. There are some things that are too important and too urgent to put off until tomorrow. There are some things that require our immediate and utmost attention.

How many times have we heard, "Sorry, too late, or "The deadline has passed, or "Time has expired." Life does not always give us a timeout to tend to urgent matters. Life does not always grant us double and triple overtime. Some things we must do now because the circumstances require immediate action. Time is the most important of all of our resources. It's the only thing we can give to others and never get back. The clock is ticking down on all of us. We must find ways of giving our immediate attention to priorities that require our utmost urgency.

Peter went with the disciples immediately and Tabitha was brought back to life. The people who loved Tabitha did not delay notifying Peter of the problem and Peter did not delay addressing the problem. They both were concerned about time. They both acted with the utmost expediency. They all had a sense of urgency in a matter of critical importance. The slightest delay could end in disaster.

There are some who believe that if Peter had come three days later, if it had been God's will, Tabitha would still have been raised. This may be true, but there is a difference between time as *chronos* and time as *kairos*. There is a difference between temporal and eternal time. We do not have forever to act on things whose resolution requires immediate attention. If someone is dying or dead, their revival time is not eternal. The revival time of the dead is both *chronos* and *kairos*. We must act within *chronos* and we must have a sense of *kairos*. We must be in time and on time in the things of God.

Ask any emergency room physician about the importance of timing in saving a life. Ask any surgeon about the value of time in doing major surgery, and you will discover that timing is virtually everything.

Too often in the things of this world we have the greatest urgency and the utmost exigency. Too often in the things of God, we are lethargic, listless, and inattentive. All too often we are inattentive to the real needs of people. We are wearied by the daily round of life which dulls our senses and slows our response time to the real things that matter in life.

The people who called Peter to Tabitha had a real sense of urgency in saving the woman's life. Peter had a sense of urgency in immediately tending to the needs of the dead woman and her family. This urgency is rooted in a compassion and concern for the well being of those we serve. In the church we are faced with crises that require a short response time to the needs of God's people. God help us if we are too long in responding to the needs of our people.

Early in my ministry at Hope United Methodist Church I learned the value of a quick response to a crisis situation. A church parishioner was dying at a local hospital and the family phoned me to come at once. "He wants to talk with you, Reverend, before he dies." I grabbed my coat, ran out of the house, and jumped into my car, but it wouldn't start. I tried to start the car for ten minutes and couldn't. I called a few friends who could not be reached. I phoned the cab company and waited another hour and no cab came. Within that time the parishioner died and the sin of my not being there was unpardonable in the minds of family members. They did not understand that I had car problems. In their minds I had failed to respond to the request of their dying loved one. They were hurt and disappointed. I felt the pangs of guilt, but it taught me the lesson that there are some things that require our immediate attention and we must come at once or go right now. This experience taught me the value of having a back-up plan in case of car failure or some other unforeseen difficulty. Now I have a person I can call who will get me where I need to be quickly.

Our preaching, counseling, pastoral care, witnessing, and discipling should have a sense of urgency. The church is too laid back. Clergy are too laid back. The body of Christ is often too laid back. There is no sense that the needs of people are vitally important. Few things are worse than tired clergy who have no compassion or concern for the needs of God's people. We must find ways of prioritizing the ultimate concerns of the people and let them know that we care for them and love them as Jesus does.

Jesus' crucifixion and resurrection dramatize the urgency of our need for salvation as God's people. The turn-around time between death and life was three days. The cycle of death and life symbolized by the crucifixion and resurrection is a short time. God did not allow Jesus to lie in the tomb forever. After the third day he arose. In the span of eternity, three days is a modicum of time. God had unfinished business for the son. The resurrection would complete this segment of Christ's mission to God's people, and that's why Christ had to get up from the grave. The Father would not let more time elapse because he had a sense of urgency in using his son as an instrument of salvation and redemption for dying and sinful people. The Father, Son, and Holy Ghost all have a sense of urgency in ministering to and saving our sin-sick souls.

The church today needs that same kind of resurrection urgency for raising the dead and meeting the needs of people. The tasks before us are compelling, if not at times overwhelming. There are so many needs, so many dying and hurting people that require our immediate attention. People must know that we care, and sometimes our caring is conveyed through our response time to their real needs.

What we need today is a resurrection urgency to bring the dead back to life. No longer must we postpone our response to the crises of our times. No longer can we simply look the other way and dismiss the importance of responding immediately to ultimate concerns because our delay can mean life or death. Perhaps in the final analysis we really do not have the power to save, heal, and resurrect, no matter how quickly or slowly we respond to people's needs, but Christ still has that power. It is through our work as servants of God that people come to know who Christ is. If we do not have a sense of urgency for our work in meeting the needs of people we might well be telling them that Christ does not have time for them. We need a resurrection urgency that will compel us to tend to the needs of a dying people.

Christ calls us now to his work now. We must sense the importance of coming at "once" because there is great need. Please come at once, the dead woman needs you.

Out Of
The Box

Acts 11:1-18

Why do some people always want to put Christians into
a tight little box? Why should we limit the gospel to people who
have heard it all before? Why shouldn't we take the gospel beyond
the four walls of the church to people who don't look like us, walk
like us, talk like us, or share our views? Why must we always talk
to the people who think like we think and do as we do? Why doesn't
our conversation and proclamation go forth to people who need to
be converted to Christ? It is true that people in the church need to
be converted, but what about those people in those neighborhoods,
environments, and conditions who are beyond our reach but who
need to hear the Good News of Christ?

Peter was confronted with the dilemma of "preaching to the
choir" or taking the message beyond the boundaries and comfort
zones believers had established for their close-knit circle. The gospel message was intended for all people and all nations, not just a
select few who are part of the spiritual inner clique.

What we have in the church today is a kind of spiritual incest,
where we have inbred a message of hope only for those with whom
we feel comfortable. We don't need zoned churches and zoned
Christians — comfort zone, safe zone, and no zone. What we need
are churches and messengers who will go beyond the conventional
boundaries and safe havens we have carved out for ourselves! It is
here that the message of God is extended into territories and terrain heretofore unexplored.

When asked why he served a poor black parish in the inner
city, a white pastor said, "Because God calls me to bring the Good
News to places where I wouldn't ordinarily go!"

It is true that humankind has an affinity for those people, places, and things with which it feels it holds the most in common. Human beings are tribal and clannish by nature. We fix ourselves in groups that reinforce our identity, safety, and comfort. We gravitate least towards those who threaten our sense of well being, make us insecure, and rattle our sense of purpose in life. We live and think and act and coexist in community with those we believe share our values and views.

The question is: Would we have the message of love and hope of Christ if Christ had stayed within the confines of his hometown? Would we be believers if those early proponents of the gospel had played it safe and never brought the Good News to people who were different?

A great tragedy today is the spiritual waste and atrophy of churches. Churches die. Churches are closed because they do not reach out to people in the surrounding neighborhoods because "those people" don't think like us or smell like us or share our views. Churches die each day because believers refuse to reach out to people who are different.

Peter was criticized for breaking bread with Gentiles, but he refused to apologize for the power and workings of God and the Holy Ghost in his life. He refused to bow to the practice self-aggrandizing idolatry, where my way of thinking is the only valid way, where my way of doing things is the only true and acceptable way. Peter refused to give in to the tyrannical forces of self-congratulation and the gospel of me-ism that is only for us. So he reached out to the Gentiles. He reached out to non-believers. He reached out to the blind, deaf, dumb, and lame. He preached the word without apology and with authority, but there were those who wanted to limit the purview of his message and his audience. The word was that they wanted him to preach only to "this" people and not to "those" people. They wanted him to limit the Good News only to those that they deemed worthy of the message.

How often do we play these games in God's church? Do we have our favorite people that we are only in mission to? Why don't more white churches have black parishioners? Why don't more black churches have white parishioners? Why don't rich churches have more poor people? Why don't more poor churches have rich people?

There is the fable of the church who placed a "for members only" sign on their front lawn. No one was ever invited to attend the church. If strangers showed up for service they were harshly turned away and discouraged from ever coming again. As the congregation aged, members began to die until finally the last three members posted a notice in the obituary column which read: Dead. Forty-five-year-old, middle-class church that once had 200 members. Address: 1888 Temple Street. Cause of death: unfriendliness towards strangers, for-members-only attitude, disdain for all people who weren't our kind of people. God forgive us for the sin of selfishness.

Peter and the apostles believed that what they had was too good to keep and that Christ did not call them to keep the Good News to themselves but to share a message of joy and hope with all people. This meant people with whom they had the least in common!

What about you and your church? Do you have an open door policy of whosoever will let him or her come? Is your church for members only? Is it a country club, a private club, where only certain people are accepted and wanted? Is the gospel preached from your pulpit a message for all people for all time or only for white people, black people, Asian people, or other kinds of people? Are you preaching to the Gentiles, the unsaved, the unredeemed, and the unforgiving and unforgiven? Have you taken the message of Christ into danger zones and others zones, or are you staying within your comfort zone?

Did Christ stay in his comfort zone? Was his ministry a comfort zone? Were the cross and crucifixion comfort zones? Were his death and resurrection places of safety and comfort? Or are you preaching a message that everybody can hear where entire households can be saved and redeemed?

Peter and the apostles refused to remain in the box that others wanted them to stay in. Peter came out of the box to bring a message of love, power, and justice to people who didn't share his views which included Jews and Gentiles.

That's what the church needs to do today. It needs to come out of the box. The box of spiritual confinement. The box of safety and comfort. The boxes of me-ism, my-ism, racism, classism, sexism and other isms. The church should come out of the box of prejudice, traditionalism, denominationalism and other boxes that stymie and stagnate the flow and presence of the Holy Ghost! You cannot put the gospel of love in a box, take it home, and hide it under your bed. You can't put the Father in a box, the Son in a box, and the Holy Ghost in a box! The Father sent the Son so we can get out of the box of sin, hatred, non-forgiveness, and other things that put us in the box in the first place. We are called to come out of the box of spiritual limitation and solitary confinement. We are called to spread the Good News of Christ to all people and not simply stay within the nice, neat little boxes we have fixed for ourselves or that others have forced us into.

Peter and the apostles refused to stay in the box. Paul refused to stay in his box. Even if Jack refuses to stay in his box, why do Christians want to stay in their boxes? Christ was crucified and resurrected so that we could come out of the box.

Jesus refused to allow hatred, prejudice, class, race, age, ethnicity, money, power, influence, sickness, affliction, trouble, sorrow, pain, or death to keep him in a box. Jesus came and died and rose so that we would come out of the box. The box of narrowmindedness and provincial thinking, the box of limited vision and opportunity and the box of the seven last words, "We never did it that way before," all kill the forward movement of the spirit's power and presence. Jesus calls us to come out of the box. The empty box is the empty tomb. Jesus is out of the box and we as disciples of Christ should come out of the box too!

When Peter saw how the Holy Ghost had come, his mission to the Gentiles was confirmed. Peter knew he had the presence and power of the Holy Ghost which emboldened him to come out of the box others tried to force him into. This is our commission, to go into the world to preach, teach, and reach others for Christ; to come out of the our little boxes to spread the Good News of Christ. We can do it when the Holy Ghost comes upon us. When we are baptized by the Holy Spirit, we can come out of the box. We no longer have to allow things to box us in and keep us from taking a message of hope to all people. Come out of your box and give him the glory!

The Hospitable Servant: A Woman Named Lydia

Acts 16:9-15

One of the great problems of our time particularly in some clergy circles is the myopic, antiquated, sexist, provincial, and prejudiced view that some pastors and congregations have regarding women in the church. This problem is particularly acute in regards to female clergy and those strong, anointed, and gifted women of God whom God has appointed and anointed for service and who also pose a threat to the fragile egos of those "true believers" who deem them unfit and unworthy to be true servants of God. We see this ignorance manifested in such foolish statements as, "God did not call women to preach. If the Lord had wanted women to serve in his church he would have called women disciples."

The problem is such vainglorious assertions cannot be corroborated by the biblical record, for it is evident that Jesus, the apostle Paul, and the other apostles and disciples had a reverence and respect for women in general and women of faith in particular. In fact, women were the mainstay of support of Jesus' movement, and there are other references throughout the Bible to women of power and strength whose faithfulness, humility, and tenacity helped to establish and solidify the early and later Christian movements. One such person was a woman called Lydia who was a true servant of God, a hospitable servant who heard the apostle preach at Phillipi in the district of Macedonia and opened her heart to him and his followers.

Lydia was a true hospitable servant of God because she heard the word of God and responded to that word with heart and soul.

Hospitable servants of God not only hear the word and are open to it but they also respond to it positively with mind, body, and soul. So much of our preaching falls on deaf ears. People listen but do not hear. People sit in the pew and go through the motions of church life, but do they really listen and do they really hear the word that issues forth? Does the word fall on rocky, stony ground and/or on fertile soil? This is a paradox of church life. We preach and proclaim, yet too often it falls on ears that are tired of hearing.

Lydia heard the word and the Lord opened her heart so she could respond to the word positively. She listened intently and accordingly responded to the Lord's plea with open arms and a willing heart. There was something in her heart and soul that resonated with the word of God. She was obviously a well-to-do merchant. Dealers in purple cloth made a good living during her time. But she was not so self-sufficient and so well-to-do that she couldn't hear and respond to the message of Paul.

Sometimes we cannot hear because we are well off. Everything is fine. No problems, worries, poverty, or afflictions. Sometimes the less we have been blessed by God the less we rely upon God and the more we are open to the promises of his word. Not Lydia. She was well off but still had a hunger and a thirst for the Good News of Christ. She was already a worshiper of God, but now she would receive a message of spiritual hope and prosperity; a word that would reach into the depths of her very soul and compel her to Christ. She heard the word of God and responded positively to it.

What a joy it is to have people listen and respond positively. They do not sit in the pew with blank and empty faces. They do not sit in the pew with blank minds and blank hearts. Their countenance does not show the scorn and scowl of the disconcerted and discontented. They do not appear to be in the twilight zone, or the never-never land of far away places. They listen intently and they respond with interest to God's word. They do not sit as diners at the table waiting to be served a full course meal of the gospel without gratitude or appreciation. Their faces are not stone, granite, and mortar devoid of life, expression, and emotion. Their hearts are opened. They sit, listen, hear, and come to Christ! What hallelujah joy and thanksgiving this brings! Of all those who truly listen, a radical minority responds positively because their hearts are opened. Lydia listened and responded with heart and soul because she opened her heart to God and the anointing of the Holy Spirit. True servants respond positively to the word of God in their lives.

Lydia was a true hospitable servant because she and her entire household were baptized and believed. A true servant reaches out to those closest to them and brings them to Christ. Not only was she baptized, but her entire household came to Christ. What a wonderful thing it is that the entire family and household can come under the influence and sway of the mighty word of God! What a joy for husbands and wives and children and others to come to Christ! It is a beautiful thing to behold, indeed, when entire families and households can come to Christ and know his joy.

Lydia was undoubtedly a woman of influence. Already a worshiper of God, she wanted more. She was a seeker of truth. Although she was a worshiper of God, she was open to new ideas and new possibilities. She may have felt that the God she served did not provide the answers she so deeply sought. Or being satisfied with her religion, she may have been compelled to Christ by the power of Paul's preaching. Whatever the case, what she experienced was so life-transforming that she became a convert to Christ. So exhilarated was she by the power and presence of the Holy Ghost that she told others in her household and they too came to Christ.

Sometimes the people in our households are the hardest to reach and convert because they see us up close and personal. They know our infirmities, iniquities, and hypocrisies. They see us without our public persona. They know our foibles and failings. Sometimes our example does not convince or compel them to Christ, for if the God we serve cannot change us, how can God change them? That Lydia was able to convince her household to Christ calls attention to the power of her positive example and the respect she had in the eyes of those who knew her and lived with her. Lydia was a true servant because she reached out to those closest to her and brought them to Christ. They were baptized and believed in Jesus. A true servant reaches out to others in the name of Jesus.

Lydia was a true hospitable servant of the Lord because she invited the messengers of God into her home. She not only accepted Christ, was baptized and believed, but also she invited the servants of God into her home.

Lydia was not content just to hear the message and go home. She invited the workers of God into her home and showed them hospitality. It is not enough to hear the word of God, and to be baptized and believe. The question is: Do we invite Christ into our homes and our hearts? Do we treat the servants of God with respect by extending hospitality to them?

Today we hear the message. We have been baptized and believe, but do we invite the servants of God into our hearts and our homes? Do we have an open door policy for Christ? Do we invite Christ and the Holy Spirit into our homes? Do we show hospitality to Christ and his servants?

One man complained after joining a well-known mega-church in Atlanta, Georgia. He was from New Jersey and had no relatives or friends in Atlanta. Believing that he could find friendship in a church, he joined, but later he was dismayed because no one ever invited him to their home. No one ever welcomed him or made him feel a sense of belonging in that church or the city. He later left the city, discouraged because there was no hospitality among the believers of that church.

It is not enough to be baptized and believe, we must show concern and hospitality for those in the body of Christ as well as those not in it. Paul and his friends were overjoyed at the invitation to come into the home of Lydia. She cared enough about them that she wanted them to experience the comforts of home after being on the road so long. They were probably tired, weary, and needed rest. She invited them home because she wanted to serve those who served God's people.

There are too many spiritual nomads, aimless wanderers; too many of the spiritually homeless who have no moorings, no resting places, no home away from home, no place where they can find rest and hospitality. The church should be the hospitality center of the community, nation, and world. It should extend a hand of welcome to the servants of God and show them hospitality wherever they are. Dorothy in the *Wizard of Oz* said, "There's no place like home." I say, "There's no place like a home away from home."

True servants of Christ extend hospitality. As long as there are churches and believers in the world there should never be spiritual homelessness. The truth is, there should never be any kind of homelessness if the church is truly a hospitality center for the community and world.

Lydia was a true servant of God because she opened her heart and responded to Christ. She reached out to her family and brought them to Christ and extended hospitality to Christ and his followers.

What we need in the world today are true servants who love the Lord and love God's people. Servants who will show joy and compassion. Servants who will help those in need and will respond with heart and soul to the Good News of Christ. It is not enough to keep the message to ourselves. It is not enough to confess and profess Christ. The true servant shares his or her faith with others and extends a grace and peace that opens the door that will invite all those who are seeking Christ into a place of comfort and rest. Lydia is a shining example of true servanthood. After opening her heart to Christ she did not hesitate to open the door of her home to those who needed comfort. True servants love God and love the people who do God's work. True servants have hospitality in their hearts. True servants believe that there are no strangers in God's world, for the road to the church should never be long. True servants open themselves to God's blessings and anointing and invite others into the Body of Christ!

You Shall Receive Power

Acts 1:1-11

Luke gives a telling account of Jesus' instructions to the apostles before his ascension into heaven. Jesus speaks to them about the kingdom of God, the importance of waiting for the gift "my father has promised," and their coming baptism by the Holy Spirit. They anxiously anticipate and question him about the restoration of the kingdom of Israel and Jesus admonishes them not to concern themselves about times or dates of the coming kingdom, but promises them that they shall receive power when the Holy Ghost descends upon them so they will be witnesses to the ends of the earth.

The power of the Holy Spirit (Holy Ghost power) is unlike any other power. It is not a power that is invented, sculpted, or demolished by human hands. It is not a power that can be manipulated for political or social purposes. It is not a power that can be manufactured, canned, and distributed like dry goods. No! The power Jesus promises is a transforming, liberating, redeeming, life-changing, and saving power that can change the course of nations and history. It is Holy Ghost power that is unlike any other power man has experienced.

"But you will receive power." Jesus does not make this a conditional imperative. He states unequivocally and absolutely: you will receive power. Power to do what? Power to rule nations? Power to dethrone Caesar? Power to vanquish forever the enemies of Israel? Power to change light into darkness? Power to restore the Kingdom of Israel to its former greatness? What kind of power is Jesus talking about?

His apostles are nervous, anxious, excited. They envision a power that will forever change their lives and those around them. They sense that a new power is permeating the air: the power of renewal and change. To possess this power would mean a new might and spiritual hegemony for them as followers of Christ.

Jesus promises this power to his followers. During his ministry he gave the disciples the power to cast out demons and heal the sick. Some of them used that power and some of them didn't. Jesus promised it then and promises it now. Only we do not accept and receive the power that he has promised to bequeath. "You will receive power." Christ promises to give that power and we must trust in him to make good on his word.

The problem is he promises it but many do not believe and never receive it. A friend of mine tells the story of how he was constantly told by his father that he would be somebody of importance when he grew up. Early in his childhood he did not believe and did not receive it. But his father kept telling him over and over that he would be somebody. Despite his poor report cards and his numerous failings as a child, his father kept confidence in him until the young man finally believed what his father told him. "You will be somebody one day! You will make a positive contribution to your community," his father would tell him. The young man finally claimed this promise of his father and later went on to become a great neurosurgeon. His father told him he would be somebody, but it wasn't until he believed it and received it that he became a person of great power.

Jesus promises that we shall receive power, but it is our disbelief that often impedes the full gust of the Spirit's anointing power in our lives. Somehow it is hard to bring ourselves to believe that this power is given to little old me. But Jesus promises it. He promised it to his apostles and promises it to his people today who have faith in him. You can't claim what has been given or promised to you if you don't have faith. If you have faith, you can believe and achieve what God has promised and then you will receive power.

When the Holy Spirit comes on you — thus the power comes when the Holy Spirit comes upon you. This is the crux, substance, core, and basis of the power. When the Holy Spirit comes upon you, the power of God will come upon you. You will have the power to preach and teach boldly in the name of Jesus, to stand up to power and principalities, to be Christ's witnesses in a world that assaults and persecutes you for your beliefs. When the Holy Ghost comes, you will receive a power you never thought you had. You will have a holy boldness, a joy, a fervor, a zeal that the world didn't give and cannot take away.

When the Holy Spirit comes upon you, stuff happens, things change, mountains move, valleys rise, troubles flee, sorrow waits, joy comes, tears wane, enemies bow, persecution is banished. When the Holy Ghost comes, the lame walk, the dumb talk, the blind see, and the deaf hear! When the Holy Ghost comes, the dead are raised, the mute shout the joy of Jesus, and the devil flees for a season. When the Holy Spirit comes upon you, the true power comes because it is a power not of the self but of God. It is a power that comes from on high and cannot be determined by things down low.

We cannot do what God calls us to do without the power, authority, leadership, anointing, and guidance of the Holy Ghost. When the Holy Ghost comes upon us, something happens inside and outside. When the Holy Ghost comes, the devil and his demons move out of the neighborhood and evil and its cohorts find other hiding places. When the Holy Ghost comes, you will receive power!

Power to do what? Power to be witnesses. Power to overcome failure. Power to vanquish sin. Power to proclaim the Good News boldly in an unreceptive world. Power to help others to Christ. It is overcoming power. Power to do the impossible. Power to succeed for Jesus against great odds. The power to dodge the arrows that fly by night and noonday and power to avert the fowler's snare. It is a power that diminishes the devastation of death, heals afflictions, casts out demons, and causes one to become whole and well again. This is the power Christ gives to those who follow and have faith in him.

There is something about Holy Ghost power that charges, renews, refreshes, and restores. There is something about Holy Ghost power that gives joy in the midst of sorrow, victory amid defeat, and sweet release from the solitary confinements of sin.

95

What the church needs today is Holy Ghost power — the power to heal, redeem, renew, and save lost souls for Christ. The church needs Holy Ghost power to proclaim boldly the Good News of Christ in a dying and crazy world. Where is the Holy Ghost power of the church? Has the Holy Ghost gone out of style? Is it now just a figment of the imagination? Do we not hear much about the Holy Ghost anymore in the church because it is no longer fashionable to be holy?

What happened to the power to say no to evil, to stand up to the enemy in ways that will encourage the saints? In an effort to be more secular than sacred and to accommodate the world, has the church compromised its Holy Ghost power?

Jesus promises that we shall receive it when the Holy Spirit comes upon us. He promises that when we receive that power we will be his witnesses in familiar and foreign, comforting and uncomforting places. But in order to receive that power, we must believe it, claim it, and achieve it by our faith in Christ.

Why do some churches close and die? Why are churches half empty instead of full? Holy Ghost power is three-pronged power: Father, Son, and Holy Ghost. Christians need the three-pronged power source. Have you noticed the difference between two-pronged and three-pronged power cords? The least little jerk on the two-pronged plug will disconnect the cord from the socket. With a three-pronged plug the cord is more firmly secured in the power socket. Some Christians don't have Holy Ghost power because they are still using two-pronged rather than three-pronged cords. The problem with other so-called Christians is that they are cordless Christians entirely. Some have two-pronged rather than three-pronged cords and others don't even have cords that will plug into their Holy Ghost power source.

Jesus says will we have power when the Holy Ghost comes upon us. In order to receive it, we must claim it and be open to be used by it for the glory of God and kingdom building.

Do you have the power to be his witness? Do you have the power to proclaim his love and truth? Do you have power to spread his message of goodness for kingdom building? Believe it and you shall receive it! Jesus promises. You shall receive power when the Holy Spirit comes upon you. Get ready, Saints, the power is coming!

Twelve O'Clock Rock:
When The Jailhouse Is Rocked

Acts 16:16-34

The prisoners and the jailers had their world rocked one midnight 2,000 years ago. The report includes the following details:

1:00: Paul and Silas while on their way to a place of prayer see a slave girl who was popular for telling the fortunes of others. She made much money from this enterprise and a fortune for her owners. Each day she would go to the town square and as people passed by she would shout out her readings of their future. Some revered the slave girl for the accuracy of her predictions. Others feared her for the same reason.

Paul and Silas saw this woman when they first entered the city several days earlier and tried to avoid her. She followed them around and said nothing. Everywhere they went she went, yet she remained silent. Now as they were again going to the place of prayer, she follows them and shouts that they are men of the most high God and that they know the way to be saved. Annoyed by her presence and the spirit inside of her, Paul turns around and calls the spirit out of her, and the spirit leaves her.

2:00: Realizing what Paul has done, the owners of the girl have words with Paul and Silas. They accuse the two of infringing on their enterprise by taking the fortune-telling spirit out of the girl. The men stand in the town square arguing with Paul and Silas, stomping their feet on the ground, pointing fingers in their faces, and threatening to kill them. The men shout for them to apologize and to make monetary amends for the money they have lost. Paul does not apologize for rebuking the spirit and calling it out. The two men stand firm, back to back. They utter a prayer in the presence of the angry men and hold their ground. The men leave vowing to come back for revenge.

3:00: The men ambush Paul and Silas as they are walking to the place of prayer. Further accusing them, slapping, beating, and kicking them to the ground, they drag the two into the town square and beat them more furiously with sticks and bricks. Crowds gather to gape at the awesome spectacle.

4:00: More friends of the owners of the slave girl come and continue their beating of Paul and Silas. Now they are dragged from the town square to the hall of the magistrate. The men continue their accusations and recriminations of Paul and Silas. Nearly unconscious from their beating, the two men can barely speak. Silas has teeth knocked out and bleeds profusely. Paul's left eye is swollen shut and he nurses a gash on his right cheek.

5:00: A fat, stinking, jolly, greasy magistrate leaps up from his chair, shaking his head in disgust, twirling a broom straw in his mouth, sucking grape wine from a jar, and watches as the crowd now joins in on the beating. After twenty more minutes of beating, kicking, spitting, cursing, and shouting, the magistrate waves the crazy crowd off and orders Paul and Silas to be officially stripped, beaten, and thrown into prison. "What we have here is a failure to communicate," growls the magistrate.

6:00: Roman centurions arrive at the scene with the flogging whips, beat the men some more, and drag them off to prison.

7:00: Arriving at the prison the captain of the guard orders the jailer to "take care of the prisoners." Here they are beaten again by the jailer and are doused with buckets of cold water.

8:00: Still in the holding area, they are now taken to their inner cells and have their hands and feet fastened in the stocks.

9:00, 10:00, and 11:00: Paul and Silas lay motionless. Paul wakes up and touches Silas to see if he is still alive. Silas moves, groans, and open his eyes. Paul thanks God that Silas is still alive and tries to give him a cup of cold water to revive him.

11:15: The two men sit up and talk. They are sore from their beatings. They petition God to forgive them for their transgressions and to forgive their transgressors. They embrace each other and cry together and begin their prayers.

11:30: Still praying, they begin shouting victory. They pray for release as the Holy Spirit descends and anoints them.

12:00: Paul and Silas begin to rock with hymns and prayers! They begin singing songs and hymns: "What A Friend We Have In Jesus" ... "Lord, I Want To Be A Christian" ... "On Christ The Solid Rock I Stand" ... "Amazing Grace" ... "Blessed Assurance" ... "His Eye Is On The Sparrow" ... "Precious Lord, Take My Hand" ... "We'll Understand It Better, Bye and Bye" ... "Leaning On The Everlasting Arms."

They alternate prayers with hymns and Holy Ghost songs. As they sing and pray, their voices get louder and stronger. A pure spiraling crescendo of a Hallelujah chorus in mezzo forte swells in the prison. As they pray and sing, they shed their wounds and pain and stand and begin to rock and sway.

They rock harder as the silence breaks! They rock stronger as the storm dikes break! They rock longer as the back of discouragement and injustice breaks! They rock wider as the prison chains break! They rock deeper as the jail bars break! They rock with a "Mississippi in the valley" rock! They rock with an "Alabama in the morning" rock! They rock with a midnight hour rock! They rock with a "Help Me, Holy Ghost" rock! They rock with a "sweet bye and bye" and a "joy cometh in the morning" rock! They rock with a "trouble don't last always" rock! They rock with a "a soon and very soon" rock!

12:00: The jailhouse rocks! They rock and sway and sing and pray as jail cell walls begin to twist, crack, dip, and split! They swing and sway, sing and shout the Holy Ghost hymns of the church and the prayers of the saints. They rock with the rock of ages. While they rock, the jailed in other cells join in the rock and the prison guards begin to roll.

12:00: The jailhouse is rocked! Hearing the music, one of the minor jailer's throws his keys in the air and does a 360 twirl and catches his keys. The other jailer does a split in the front office and starts singing "Oh, happy day!" The other jailers begin running every which way like they don't know the time of day!

99

As they rock, a violent earthquake begins to rumble, and the walls begin to tumble. The doors fly open. Teeth shudder. The chains come loose at 12:00 and the jailer is roused by what he sees! Fearing for his life, he grabs his sword and tries to kill himself. But Paul and Silas caution him to spare his own life because "the prisoners are all here."

Through songs and prayers and faith and the Holy Ghost, the jailhouse was rocked and the chief jailer was so shook up by what he saw that he asked what he must do to be saved. And as things settled down, they began to speak to him about the power and joy of the Lord. So rocked was the jailer that he washed their wounds and he and his entire household were baptized and saved. The jailer invited the men into his home and the magistrate ordered them released. Because they were Roman citizens, they would not walk out of the jail on their own. They demanded Roman escorts because of the way they had been mistreated.

The jailhouse was rocked at midnight and the prisoners were set free. The truth is, Paul and Silas were already free men although they were in chains. Their faith, perseverance, tenacity, and joy could not be vanquished by their surroundings. They were men of great faith whose prayers and hymns had so much power that the jailhouse was rocked at its foundations.

Have you ever had your world rocked to the point where things just fell apart? Have you ever been rocked by injustice, evil, oppression, sin, and other forms of iniquity? Have you ever found yourself in what appeared to be an impossible situation? After you have been beaten, mistreated, given up for dead, and thrown into jail, did God make a way out of no way? Did walls that held you in come tumbling down because of your great faith?

Has ill treatment from others ever caused you to live out your life in the solitary cells of hell and unhappiness? Know that whatever your situation, condition, imprisonment, confinement, restriction, God can rock that situation and bring about a change for the better. There is nothing that prayer and praise cannot change. If they do not change our condition they can certainly change our outlook and response to our condition.

This is our faith in Christ. A faith that will rock the very foundations of our various forms of imprisonment. A faith that will rock our enemies and the very confinements in which they try to place us and keep us. God can rock the foundations of injustice and untruth and will bring victory and joy to those imprisoned by iniquity. However great the injustice, however cruel and diabolical the enemy, God will rock the foundations of our imprisonments and abolish the pain of our solitary confinement. God will rock untruth with truth, hatred with love, evil with good. He is a Rock of Ages who can rock every fortress of sin and evil to bring release and freedom to those who trust him. Let us sing our songs and pray our prayers until the walls of imprisonment come tumbling down! This is the meaning of the "Twelve O'Clock Rock!"

Books In This Cycle C Series

GOSPEL SET

Praying For A Whole New World
Sermons For Advent/Christmas/Epiphany
William G. Carter

Living Vertically
Sermons For Lent/Easter
John N. Brittain

Changing A Paradigm — Or Two
Sermons For Sundays After Pentecost (First Third)
Glenn E. Ludwig

Topsy-Turvy: Living In The Biblical World
Sermons For Sundays After Pentecost (Middle Third)
Thomas A. Renquist

Ten Hits, One Run, Nine Errors
Sermons For Sundays After Pentecost (Last Third)
John E. Berger

FIRST LESSON SET

The Presence In The Promise
Sermons For Advent/Christmas/Epiphany
Harry N. Huxhold

Deformed, Disfigured, And Despised
Sermons For Lent/Easter
Carlyle Fielding Stewart III

Two Kings And Three Prophets For Less Than A Quarter
Sermons For Sundays After Pentecost (First Third)
Robert Leslie Holmes

What If What They Say Is True?
Sermons For Sundays After Pentecost (Middle Third)
John W. Wurster

A Word That Sets Free
Sermons For Sundays After Pentecost (Last Third)
Mark Ellingsen

SECOND LESSON SET
You Have Mail From God!
Sermons For Advent/Christmas/Epiphany
Harold C. Warlick, Jr.

Hope For The Weary Heart
Sermons For Lent/Easter
Henry F. Woodruff

A Hope That Does Not Disappoint
Sermons For Sundays After Pentecost (First Third)
Billy D. Strayhorn

Big Lessons From Little-Known Letters
Sermons For Sundays After Pentecost (Middle Third)
Kirk W. Webster

Don't Forget This!
Robert R. Kopp
Sermons For Sundays After Pentecost (Last Third)